Apostolic Foundations

by
Art Katz

BURNING BUSH PRESS
BEMIDJI, MINNESOTA, USA

APOSTOLIC FOUNDATIONS

by Art Katz

Copyright © 2009—Art Katz Ministries

All rights reserved. This book is protected under the copyright laws of the United States of America and may not be copied or reprinted for commercial gain or profit. The use of short quotations or occasional page copying for personal or group study is permitted and encouraged.

Unless otherwise stated, Scripture quotations are taken from the NEW AMERICAN STANDARD BIBLE®, Copyright © 1960, 1962, 1963, 1968, 1971, 1972, 1973, 1975, 1977, 1995 by the Lockman Foundation. Used by permission. www.Lockman.org.

KJV is the King James Version of the Bible, copyright © 1972 by Thomas Nelson Inc. and published by Thomas Nelson Publishers).

These and other materials of a comparable kind can be found at: www.artkatzministries.org

First Edition: ISBN 981-04-2481-7

Second American Edition, 2009

ISBN 10 digit: 0-9749631-7-8
ISBN 13 digit: 978-0-9749631-7-4

Published by Burning Bush Press

About The Author

Art Katz was born in Brooklyn, New York, of Jewish parents, and raised during the Great Depression and turbulence of World War II. Dropping out of high school, Art became a merchant seaman, and was later drafted into the Army and stationed in post-war Germany. He later taught at an Oakland high school. Shattered by the disillusionment and horror of the Holocaust perpetrated against his Jewish kinsmen, Art embraced Marxist and existentialist ideologies as the solution to the vexing human predicament.

Hitchhiking through Europe and the Middle East while on a leave-of-absence from the teaching profession, the cynical and unbelieving atheist, anti-religionist and anti-Christian, was radically apprehended by a God who was actively seeking him. The actual journal of that experience, *Ben Israel – Odyssey of a Modern Jew*, recounts Art's quest for the true meaning to life, which climaxed significantly and symbolically in Jerusalem.

Art attended Santa Monica City College, UCLA, and the University of California at Berkeley, earning Bachelor's and Master's degrees in history, as well as a Master's degree in theology at Luther Seminary, St. Paul, Minnesota. With his speaking ministry spanning nearly forty years, Art sought to bring the radical relevance of the Bible's message to contemporary societies, both secular and religious. With several of his books translated into major foreign languages, Art traveled frequently and widely as a conference speaker and prophetic voice for the Church until his death in 2007.

Acknowledgments

Art Katz was a prolific speaker, and the contents of this book are comprised exclusively from transcriptions of spoken messages. Rather than a correctly phrased literary production, we have sought to blend approved editing principles with the desire for the reader to "hear" the spirit and voice of the speaker as they read the book.

Our appreciation goes out to the many who helped with this task. Special thanks to Linda Dunaway for her monumental labors in the careful transcribing of many of the messages that make up the manuscript. Thomas Lei had an exceptional burden for the message of the book, and provided much needed help in editing and proofing the manuscript. A special thanks to Chuck Schmitt for providing the cover graphic design.

Having gone through six printings in its first edition, some further needful editing work has been done, including the addition of a previously published booklet entitled: Apostolic Conversion. We thus have the second edition of what has become Art's most popular book.

With the second edition published posthumously, we feel that Art would have wanted to dedicate this book to those who would leave no stone unturned in seeking to reclaim the apostolic foundations of the faith, so vibrant at the church's inception, and needing again to be restored.

Simon Hensman
Laporte, MN
June 2009

Apostolic Foundations

TABLE OF CONTENTS

Introduction.. 8

Chapter 1.. 23
APOSTOLIC SERVICE: PRIESTLINESS
The Levitical Consecration • The Anointing Oil • The Sacrifice • Obedience • Waiting in Silence • True Blessing • The Glory of God • As the Priest, so also the People • The Call to Priesthood • The Melchizedek Priesthood • Seated In Heaven • The Holy of Holies • Within the Veil • Saved to the Uttermost! • Summary

Chapter 2.. 65
APOSTOLIC PERCEPTION: ETERNITY
Seeing the Unseen • An Apostolic Distinctive • Strangers in the World • Eternity and Resurrection Life • True Biblical Faith • The Promises of God • Our True Dwelling Place • The Afflictions of the Saints • The Eternal Mindset • Eternal Reward • The Two Resurrections • The Judgment Seat of Christ • The Millennial Kingdom • The Invisible Cloud of Witnesses • Entering His Rest • Excommunication • The Apocalyptic View and the 'Blessed Hope' of the Church • Mockers and Scoffers in the Last Days • Apocalyptic Scenario

Chapter 3 123
APOSTOLIC REALITIES: THE PRINCIPALITIES &
POWERS OF THE AIR
The Fall • The Cosmic Setting • The Clash of Two
Wisdoms • The World as System • The Theocratic
Context • The Final Defeat • The Power of the
Cross • The Meaning of the Cross • The Provision
of God in Fellowship • The Power of True Praise •
The Manifold Wisdom of God • The Overcoming
of the Saints • Conclusion

Chapter 4 161
APOSTOLIC PROCLAMATION
The Word of the Cross • True Preaching Waits on
True Sending • Resurrection Life • The Voice of the
Preacher • Our Preaching Mandate • Come Up and
Be There!

Chapter 5 179
APOSTOLIC CONFRONTATION
The Inception of Paul's Message • The Essence of
Idolatry • Ultimate Confrontation • God as Creator
and Lord • God the Giver • The Nations in Paul's
Message • The Purpose of Man's Existence • The
Purpose of Nations • The Nations in Relation to
Israel • The Heart of Paul's Message • The Nations
in the Light of Judgment • Resurrection—The
Power of Paul's Message • The Finality of Paul's
Message

Chapter 6 205
APOSTOLIC CHARACTER
Humility and Obedience • The Broken Alabaster
Vial • Meekness: The Key to Revelation • The Two
Witnesses • Blameless Consistency • Conclusion

Chapter 7..223
APOSTOLIC CONVERSION
A study of Saul's conversion on the road to Damascus.

INTRODUCTION

The Anatomy of Apostolic

The Lord designates Himself as the Apostle of our confession,[1] and therefore I have a very special respect for anything that has to do with the word "apostolic." Apostolic reality is at the heart of the faith, but it is not a word that is easy to define. It is an ultimate word, pulsating with glory. It is a word that needs to be resuscitated, rather than to be thought of merely as a denominational identification. Like every great biblical word, we need to be apprehended by the essence of what that word represents.

Apostolic brings to mind the heart and spirit of the early church when it was at its glory, when it was authentic and vital. Indeed, only an apostolic church can stand and overcome in the perilous last days, and by that witness, testify to an obdurate and resistant

---

[1] See Hebrews 3:1

remnant of Israel in the mystery of God at the end of this age.[2]

If the church is built upon the foundation of the apostles and prophets,[3] then we need to appropriate the meaning of that reality in order to come into the intention of God and convey that reality to the world. We need, therefore, to earnestly seek the apostolic foundations of the faith, or we will not have a church worthy of that name. A church with apostolic foundations is that body of people whose central impulse and principle of life and service is a total jealousy for the glory of God. Nothing of any eternal consequence can be accomplished in the earth independent of a church that has these foundations.

The root of the Greek word *apostolos* is a "sent one." That which is not sent of God cannot accomplish the purposes of God. He empowers only what He sends, and we are going to examine the anatomy of sending from the account of the commissioning and sending of Moses when he encountered God in the burning bush. All the timeless principles of God that have to do with apostolic foundations are found in that encounter.

> Now Moses was pasturing the flock of Jethro his father-in-law, the priest of Midian; and he led the flock to the west side of the wilderness and came to Horeb, the mountain of God.
>
> The angel of the LORD appeared to him in a blazing fire from the midst of a bush; and

---

[2] See Author's book: *The Mystery of Israel and the Church* for a fuller understanding of the mystery.

[3] See Ephesians 2:19-21

he looked, and behold, the bush was burning with fire, yet the bush was not consumed.

So Moses said, "I must turn aside now and see this marvelous sight, why the bush is not burned up."

When the LORD saw that he turned aside to look, God called to him from the midst of the bush and said, "Moses, Moses!" And he said, "Here I am."

Then He said, "Do not come near here; remove your sandals from your feet, for the place on which you are standing is holy ground."

He said also, "I am the God of your father, the God of Abraham, the God of Isaac, and the God of Jacob." Then Moses hid his face, for he was afraid to look at God.

The LORD said, "I have surely seen the affliction of My people who are in Egypt, and have given heed to their cry because of their taskmasters, for I am aware of their sufferings.

"So I have come down to deliver them from the power of the Egyptians, and to bring them up from that land to a good and spacious land, to a land flowing with milk and honey, to the place of the Canaanite and the Hittite and the Amorite and the Perizzite and the Hivite and the Jebusite.

"Now, behold, the cry of the sons of Israel has come to Me; furthermore, I have seen the oppression with which the Egyptians are oppressing them.

"Therefore, come now, and I will send you to Pharaoh, so that you may bring My people, the sons of Israel, out of Egypt."

But Moses said to God, "Who am I, that I should go to Pharaoh, and that I should bring the sons of Israel out of Egypt?"

And He said, "Certainly I will be with you, and this shall be the sign to you that it is I who have sent you: when you have brought the people out of Egypt, you shall worship God at this mountain."

Then Moses said to God, "Behold, I am going to the sons of Israel, and I will say to them, 'The God of your fathers has sent me to you.' Now they may say to me, 'What is His name?' What shall I say to them?"

God said to Moses, "I AM WHO I AM"; and He said, "Thus you shall say to the sons of Israel, 'I AM has sent me to you.' "

God, furthermore, said to Moses, "Thus you shall say to the sons of Israel, 'The LORD, the God of your fathers, the God of Abraham, the God of Isaac, and the God of Jacob, has sent me to you.' This is My name forever, and this is My memorial-name to all generations."[4]

The word *sent* is used five times, and we are therefore given an insight into both the God who sends and the one who is sent. For example, why did this

---
[4] Exodus 3:1-15

episode take place on the back side (west side) of the desert, and why was there a forty-year preparation in the wilderness that preceded it? Why did God wait for Moses to turn aside and see *before* He called him? What if Moses had not turned aside to see? Could this turning aside be the pivotal and critical turning point? God did not *tell* Moses to turn aside to see. Something from the man himself was needful, and if God does not find that same thing in us, we will not come into an apostolic reality.

There is a parallel between the commissioning of Paul and the commissioning of Moses. They were both great master-builders who facilitated the purposes of God for their generation. Forty years earlier and out of his own self-initiated conduct, Moses had sought to deliver his people from Egyptian bondage. It eventuated in the death of one Egyptian, hastily buried in the sand, and Moses was required to flee into the wilderness. When the moment of encounter came, the true fulfillment of his calling was given.

To what degree, therefore, must failure precede a true appropriation of one's calling? It was certainly true for Paul and Moses. In all of our wishful intentions to serve God, are we willing for the humiliation of failure, allowed and established by God Himself? God forms a man whom He can send only out of the debris, the death and the mortification of *that* failure. There is something about failure that does a necessary, deep work in the human soul like nothing else can. The fact that we have not experienced failure is more than likely a statement that we have not had apostolic intention.

There was a largesse of soul that was to be seen in

both Paul and Moses before their conversions. Neither of them was satisfied with the *status quo*. In both of them, there was an intensity of heart to serve God. When God finds such a one as that, even in his own error, then there is more potential for him than for those who purport to be His friends, but who have not that intensity, and would rather drift along, preferring to live lackluster lives. Peter also failed dismally, but a great apostle came forth from that humiliating failure.

> Now it came about in those days, when Moses had grown up, that he went out to his brethren and looked on their hard labors; and he saw an Egyptian beating a Hebrew, one of his brethren.
>
> So he looked this way and that, and when he saw there was no one around, he struck down the Egyptian and hid him in the sand.[5]

Though Moses was called of God, he was not yet qualified to be a deliverer. He lacked the fear of God and the awareness of God. His whole posture was horizontal; he looked this way and that, and he acted, but he did not consider looking up. Merely because we see something that needs to be rectified is not the justification for us to correct it. There is nothing more opposed to the purposes of God than the well-wishing intentions that men perpetrate out of their own human and religious zeal. We will never be sent of God so long as we are motivated to act in response to need. Moses is sent because *God* heard the cry of the sons of Israel; He saw their affliction and prepared a man to be

---

[5] Exodus 2:11-12

sent to them as deliverer.

Under the Aaronic priesthood, the priests did not commence their priestly ministry until seven days of waiting were fulfilled. Seven is the number of completion, and the completion for them was the final death of their intentions to do for God. Until *that* dies, there is no true priestly service, and if it is not priestly, then it is not apostolic. Jesus is also the High Priest of our confession.[6] Any impatience, self-will, religious ambition, the compulsion to do for God, and the need to be recognized and acknowledged, will never be a glory unto God.

In his eightieth year, when God confronts Moses at the burning bush and sends him, Moses says, "Who am I that I should go?" He is a broken man, one who has been truly emptied of all of his human qualifications, which are supreme and sublime. His genealogy was derived from the priestly tribe, and also being a prince of Egypt, he was versed in all of their wisdom and knowledge.

However, Moses is now a man who has not a wit of confidence that he can perform anything, let alone deliver an entire people out of bondage. The whole preliminary work of God is to disqualify us before we can be qualified. This is totally contrary to the whole religious mindset and spirit of the world, who would see this process as absolutely wasteful, because, after all, here is a man who, at the age of forty, is full of vigor and ready to do great things for God. How many of us are itching to go out and make our mark for God? And yet God does not think it lavish, wasteful, or

---

[6] See Hebrews 3:1

extravagant to give Moses another forty years of waiting in the wilderness until he is completely emptied out, and *then* God calls him.

While God waited an additional forty years for Moses to come to maturity, Israel continued to be afflicted an additional forty years. God did not count that as being wasteful or unmerciful. In other words, God allowed an entire nation to suffer mistreatment while He waited for the moment when He would act. What do you think of a God like that? Do we know God in *that* way? Until we do, how shall we be sent, for how will we represent Him and make Him known if we do not know Him as He is? An apostle is sent in the place of another. He is representing God, the substance of what He is in Himself. That is an expensive knowledge when one considers the amount of Jewish suffering that took place in the waiting, and yet God allowed it. Contrast that to human nature, which is essentially expedient and utilitarian in what it wants to do. It performs what needs to be performed as soon as it appropriately can. However, God is timeless and eternal, and has a far different view about human suffering than we; and He will not send someone as deliverer who is half-baked in the understanding of Himself.

Having the true knowledge of God is what makes an apostle foundational to the church. That knowledge is not cheap; it takes years to obtain at the hand of God through trials, suffering and failures. If we have subscribed to a superficial, intellectual understanding of God, and have not wrestled with the righteousness of God and the judgments of God, and why He allows suffering, then we will not be sent. We need rather to burrow in to understand the enigma of God, and not to be satisfied with mere credal statements. Many of us are not being sent because we have been satisfied with a patsy notion of God, which may be technically correct, but is not, in fact, true.

Is it a coincidence that Moses is *forty* years on the back side of the desert? The number "forty" signifies trial and testing. An extraordinary preparation of a man for service is required. Will we be willing to submit to conditions of trial and preparation for true service, especially when those around us are clamoring for action and missions' activity?

Moses was a shepherd all those years, and there is something in God's heart that is tenderly disposed to those who watch the flock by night, who are dutiful, faithful and unprepossessing. There was nothing lower in Egyptian values than tending flocks, and for forty years that was all Moses did. The purposes of God are served in the formation of His servants when they give themselves to labor that is monotonous and predictable, that lacks any kind of flamboyance or charismatic excitement, but requires a steadfast patience and faithful performance, day after day. If Moses had not done that, he would not have been qualified to bring the flock of God out of Egypt. The one was a necessary preliminary for the other, and we need to serve *our* apprenticeship in the things that are ordinary, unseen and undistinguished. We need to show ourselves faithful in those places so that we can be faithful in the true works of God. This is the sublime wisdom and requirement of God. For Moses, it came out of circumstances: fleeing from Egypt, and finding himself in Midian, and into an economy that had at its heart the tending of sheep. It was God's perfect and necessary preparation for a man who had been a prince in Egypt.

Moses led the flock on the *back side* of the desert where the mount of God is to be found. We can go to our charismatic conferences with all of their renowned speakers promising great "experiences with God," and yet come back with ashes in our mouth because we have gone to the front side rather than the back. The mount of God is not located *there*. Horeb means "dry, barren and impoverished." *That* is the mount of God, and it is *there* that He is to be found. Do we have a stomach to seek Him in that place? The back side is unsavory, unbecoming and unspectacular. The front side seems to be where the action is; it has all the glitter, the big names, the impressive programs and buildings, but the whole environment is not conducive to seeking God.

All that I have been saying are the preliminary qualifications for the encounter with God, out of which will come the true sending. Mt. Horeb is a lowly, insignificant mount, which is not only *where* God is found, but also *what* God is in Himself. It is for the very same reason that He was born in a stable. This is *God*, and it is this knowledge of God that brings men out of the bondage of Egypt. Egypt is the antithesis of the desert. Egypt is a picture of the world in its lush carnality and fleshly gratification. God is found at Mt. Horeb, the place of dryness, seeming disappointment and nothing that tantalizes the flesh. God is the God of humility, and it is only the revelation of God's humility that can save men out of Egypt. The rejected and visibly inferior place is alone calculated to destroy the thing that has impressive outward credentials. The weakness of God is greater than the strength of men, and the foolishness of God is greater than the wisdom of men. Egypt was the epitome of human wisdom and civilization, but Mt. Horeb is something entirely opposite.

The man whom God reserves for authentic use is going to confront very Pharaoh himself in an ultimate demonstration, rather than a few Egyptians. God does hear the cry of the afflicted, and does see their need. But we have to have a sublime confidence, not only in His compassion and mercy, but also in His sovereignty, that we might be spared from self-initiated activity and from becoming premature "saviors" of the world.

> The angel of the LORD appeared to him in a blazing fire from the midst of a bush; and he looked, and behold, the bush was burning with fire, yet the bush was not consumed.
>
> So Moses said, "I must turn aside now and see this marvelous sight, why the bush is not burned up."
>
> When the LORD saw that he turned aside to look, God called to him from the midst of the bush and said, "Moses, Moses!" And he said, "Here I am."[7]

Why did God choose a bush instead of revealing Himself to Moses in an apparition form as He did to Joshua? What does God want to impress on our minds by this kind of revelation of Himself? What is there in

---

[7] Exodus 3:2-4

a burning bush that reveals God? Was Moses' turning aside to see a voluntary act of his will? Or was it mere curiosity? What did he see that evoked this uttermost consecration of himself to God: "Here I am"? Will God send anyone of a lesser consecration?

A desert bush is the most ordinary, scrubby thing that can be found. Would it not have been more appropriate for God to have been in the midst of some great towering oak that bespeaks the grandeur of God? If we have not found God where He is most profoundly to be discovered, it is because we have not thought to find Him in the most unlikely and ordinary thing. There is a revelation of God that can only be given in that place, or we cannot be sent. When we will turn aside to see God in *that* bush, then God calls. An apostolic person is one who sees the grandeur of God in the ordinary place and the ordinary circumstance. We tend to look for the impressive, but God is in the grit of daily life, in its failures, frustrations and vexations. God is found right in the midst of the trials of our life, and if we have not thought to find Him there, then we have not yet found Him in truth.

The extraordinary preparation of the apostolic man can only be understood in the eternal perspective, not only in this age, but also in the ages to come. Unless we understand the eternal context, we will not be willing to patiently submit to the preparation of our character. Our call is an eternal call, and our earthly service is only one aspect of that fulfillment. God sees everything in the eternal context, and that is why forty and eighty years are nothing in His sight. Everything on earth is preparation for the ages to come; and everything we are about needs to be seen in this context.

Moses turned aside to see, but how many of us would have simply passed it by? God looks to the man or woman who will turn aside to see, to those who will seek to examine their past failures and every previous, lowly aspect of their lives. If we are only looking for something large, something magnificent, something heroic and dramatic, we will not find God there; we will not even hear His call.

If there is a fellowship of believers that languishes in its superficiality, looking for something outside of itself to spice up its services, it will never find God. The things that make up the grit of its life are the very places where God abides and dwells. If we would look into that grit, and give ourselves to examine it, we would find such unspeakable realms of meaning and significance, even very God Himself, in a depth that we would not otherwise have found. How can we ever serve the purposes of God when we have not even examined the content of our own life? How many of us love looking for biblical truths but neglect to look into the grit of the things that constitute our normal daily life?

This turning aside to look into what we would otherwise have dismissed is a key to our whole future use in God. In God's sight, that which is past is now, and God requires that which is past.[8] Humanly speaking, the past is the very thing we want to overlook because it is a painful looking. We do not want to remember things that have to do with failure,

---

[8] See Ecclesiastes 3:15

with divorces, with abortions, lost friendships, and everything else that tears the fabric of life. When Moses turned aside to see, it was not mere human curiosity wanting to understand an aberration of nature, but rather a man turning aside to get *into* something.

How much of our church life is nothing more than a succession of services, with choruses, sermons and programs that serve as an overlay for a people who are struggling and failing inside? The church will never be an apostolic reality until it turns back and deals with the grit of its life. Merely to adopt a new vocabulary of apostolic terms is to compound the error. We have got enough raw material and treasure in God's people in the ordinary constitution of their lives, their circumstances and their histories, that if we would but examine it, and deal with it, we would have the key to apostolic glories.

When we will turn aside to see, we will say goodbye to our categories and convictions of what and who we thought God was. To turn aside to see means that something fundamental has turned, and there is of necessity no going back. We need to be willing to take that risk. All of our security, both natural and spiritual, all of the things that we have understood about the faith, or ourselves in the faith, might well be lost, and indeed, it *needs* to be lost. Unless we are willing to risk the loss of all things, there will be no calling, there will be no sending.

God called Moses' name twice. In most instances through the scriptures, men who are called twice are called to something of great consequence, requiring their all. As absolute and total as God's call, so equally was Moses' answer: "Here I am." This is at the heart of *apostolic*; namely, no strings attached, no holds barred, no conditions and no reservations. The presence of God, the call of God, and the total response of the man make that ground holy.

If this book is anything, it is a call to this ground, to this foundation; namely, the knowledge of God as He is and desires to be made known. May these great apostolic themes kindle in your own hearts nothing less or other than this holy standard. And may something come into the marrow of your being that henceforth will never let you go.

CHAPTER 1

Apostolic Service: Priestliness

> Therefore, holy brethren, partakers of a heavenly calling, consider Jesus, the Apostle and High Priest of our confession.[1]

There is an inexorable connection between the *apostolic* and the *priestly*. If priestliness is just a fanciful term that has little or no meaning for us, then our service for God will be equally nondescript. Priests bring the sense of heaven into the earth-bound world. Another synonym for heaven is *reality*. Whatever reality is, then that is heaven, but it takes a priestly mentality to sense that, and to feel for that, and a priestly ministry to introduce that in a world that is inhospitable to heaven.

---

[1] Hebrews 3:1

If someone had asked me as a troubled and perplexed kid, trying to make sense out of a bewildering universe, what I thought my true vocation was, or to what I thought I was called to, I knew, even in my atheistic ignorance, that the real answer, if I had the courage to speak it, was "Priest."

The Levitical Consecration

For a long time, I had considered any teaching on the priestly garments and procedures pertaining to priesthood to be quite dull, but I am now convinced that there is an eternal weight of glory in everything that has to do with priesthood. Priestliness must both precede and accompany the apostolic walk. We urgently need God to breathe upon us the spirit of true priesthood, thereby transforming every aspect of our lives, our walk and our ministry. There is a requirement to minister unto God *before* one ministers to men. If we lack the sense of the sacredness of God, then there is going to be something brittle, something lacking, something plastic in the ministry we bring.

Leviticus Chapter 8 describes the consecration of the priests. One cannot but sense the strange and antique ring about the whole process. It seems so altogether remote from anything that can be considered modern. One is tempted to hurriedly pass over it as something rightfully buried in antiquity, no longer needing any claim upon our attention. However, *everything* in this chapter is profoundly relevant for our generation, perhaps even more relevant for us than it was for the biblical generation to which it was addressed. This is not an academic consideration of the obscure practices of Old Testament priesthood; rather it is <u>God rubbing our faces into t</u>he grit of <u>apostolic real</u>ity.

The chapter begins with: "Then the Lord spoke to Moses…" and follows on with: "As the Lord commanded Moses…As the Lord commanded Moses…As the Lord commanded Moses." Right from that beginning, God wants to direct our minds to the <u>divine origin</u> of all that is to follow. These requirements could not have had their origin in human contemplation. The whole concept is totally divine, a calculated attack upon human sensibility and good taste, and is, therefore, all the more valuable and revealing.

One experiences a certain sense of exhaustion just from the reading of this chapter. What then must have been the effect of actually participating in the fulfillment of all of these requirements of God? All of the cutting, the sprinkling of the blood, the wave offerings and the sitting at the door of the tent of meeting seem absurd and arduous. By the time it was all finished, and those blood-bespattered men were waiting at the door of the tent of meeting, anything appealing and honorific to the flesh about the role of priest would have dimmed and paled. This will cure us from romantic notions of what priestly means.

> Then the LORD spoke to Moses, saying, "Take Aaron and his sons with him, and the garments and the anointing oil and the bull of the sin offering, and the two rams and the basket of unleavened bread, and assemble all the congregation at the

doorway of the tent of meeting."²

The whole congregation of Israel was required to observe the entire process as a living instruction, and therefore they had an advantage that we do not have; we do not see animals being cut up, or see the absurdity of catching the blood in basins and sprinkling it upon articles of furniture, upon the clothing of the priests and upon their ear, thumb and big toe. To the one who is observing this process, something has got to register upon his deepest consciousness about the <u>meaning of sin and what is required to expiate</u> it. Someone had to stand between God and man. Death had to be performed in order to release the life-giving provision.

There is a Melchizedek priesthood, a <u>royal priesthood</u>, but God intends that <u>we understand what preceded and foreshadowed it</u> in the Old Testament. The essentials of priesthood, the deepest meanings given to priesthood at the very beginning, are subsumed and taken into the final configuration at the last.

> So Moses did just as the LORD commanded him. When the congregation was assembled at the doorway of the tent of meeting, Moses said to the congregation, "This is the thing which the LORD has commanded to do." Then Moses had Aaron and his sons come near and washed them with water. He put the tunic on him and girded him with the sash, and clothed him with the robe and put the ephod on him; and he girded him

---

² Leviticus 8:1-3

> with the artistic band of the ephod, with which he tied it to him. He then placed the breastpiece on him, and in the breastpiece he put the Urim and the Thummin.³

How much are we willing to be stripped and washed in the water of the Word? How willing are we to endure the humiliation of nakedness before men, before even the first priestly garment can be put on? Moses washed Aaron and his sons *before* the garments were donned. It was a public humiliation, and all Israel was watching the preliminaries of their consecration. Humiliation is at the heart of priesthood. The garments were attached to the priests with skillfully woven cords. This was no quick on-and-off backstage costume change. Priesthood is not a role to be performed behind the pulpit, and then discarded upon returning home. It is not a calling that a man chooses because he thinks it is appealing; there is an exacting preparation that is not to be entered into lightly.

> He also placed the turban on his head, and on the turban, at its front, he placed the golden plate, the holy crown, just as the LORD had commanded Moses.⁴

Resting upon Aaron's forehead was a golden plate with the words, "Holiness unto the Lord" inscribed on it. With every step and every gesture, that plate would have registered its presence against his skin. We need that constant reminder, because our head is always wanting opportunity, if we would grant it, to have its own excursions, its own delights, its own activities and

---
³ Ibid., vv.4-8
⁴ Leviticus 8:9

its own thoughts. The mind continually needs to be brought back to the knowledge of a holy God. There would be much less brash and soulish ministry, and much less of a rush to come to the place of speaking, if that golden weight were resting squarely between our eyes. Only after being thus clothed, and thus prepared, did the priest receive the anointing oil.

THE ANOINTING OIL

> Moses then took the anointing oil and anointed the tabernacle and all that was in it, and consecrated them.[5]

If ever a subject deserves examination, it is the phenomenon of anointing. Very expensive ingredients were required to make it up, and there was an *extreme* penalty for anyone who made something that approximated to the holy anointing oil. The ingredients or spices were usually associated with the anointing of a body for burial. They had a very particular fragrance, and were not to be employed for the things that have to do with the purposes of men.

We can say much about fictitious anointing, things that seem to be like it and are not, but are more the overflow of human personality. How many of us can distinguish between our own human personality and the holy anointing of God? There are pastors and preachers operating today who have the gift of the gab, or an administrative ability, or are masters at conducting a service, but that is not the operation of the anointing. God will not force upon us the perfect if

---

[5] Ibid., v.10

we are satisfied with the counterfeit. But when we spurn the man-made thing, and rest wholly upon what *God* gives, then we are candidates to receive the true anointing of God.

As far back as the 1920's, Watchman Nee warned the church that the deadliest deception of the last days was the soulish substitute for the realm of Spirit that would come through technology and music. We need to guard against anything that initiates emotional response in us, lest we find ourselves depending upon soul power rather than the power of the Spirit of God. The anointing of God can be simulated in the way we modulate our tone of voice, or use it as a technological instrument to bring about a certain response. Every time we turn the amplifiers up, or give our voices a little soulish boost and add a little razzmatazz in order to bring an effect, or give an invitation that we know is calculated to play upon the emotional responses of our hearers, then *that* is false anointing; it is making something like it.

THE SACRIFICE

> He sprinkled some of it on the altar seven times and anointed the altar and all its utensils, and the basin and its stand, to consecrate them. Then he poured some of the anointing oil on Aaron's head and anointed him, to consecrate him. Next Moses had Aaron's sons come near and clothed them with tunics, and girded them with sashes and bound caps on them, just as the LORD had commanded Moses. Then he

> brought the bull of the sin offering, and Aaron and his sons laid their hands on the head of the bull of the sin offering. Next Moses slaughtered it.[6]

The slaughtering of the bull by Moses was a horrific phenomenon, a bringing to death in order that there might be life. It was done before *the entire congregation*; they watched the knife go in, and watched as the blood spurt out. They saw the animal sag, totter and go down, and then saw it being cut up. In all the blood and gore, one cannot tell where the priest ends and the sacrifice begins; *for the priest and the sacrifice have become one.*

> And [Moses] took the blood and with his finger put some of it around on the horns of the altar, and purified the altar. Then he poured out the rest of the blood at the base of the altar and consecrated it, to make atonement for it. He also took all the fat that was on the entrails and the lobe of the liver, and the two kidneys and their fat; and Moses offered it up in smoke on the altar. But the bull and its hide and its flesh and its refuse, he burned in the fire *outside the camp*, just as the LORD had commanded Moses.[7]

This is the opposite of what man would have done, which shows how much heaven is antithetical to earthly reckoning and consideration. We would have saved the things that God commands to be destroyed, and those things that we would have cast aside as

---

[6] Leviticus 8:11-15a
[7] Ibid., vv.15b-17

disgusting and worthless are the very things that *God* calls the sacrifice. The flesh and the hide, which *we* would have deemed as having great value, were burnt outside the camp; such is God's disgust for flesh.

The things that are a sweet savor to God are the inner parts, not the outward things. The work of God in the inner man, in the hidden places, in the things that are born in inward wrestling, are the offerings that please Him. If we offer our personalities, our winsomeness and our fleshly abilities to God, it is because we do not have the inward parts to offer, never having learned to rest or wait before God. The offerings that are sweet to God are formed deep within us when we bear the sufferings and reproach of the cross; these are the things that God esteems.

A true priest is one who has an accumulation of the inward workings of God in the hidden place; He knows God behind the veil of circumstances and outward feelings. God has dealt with him in ways that cannot always be explained to men, ways that leave the man utterly alone to suffer and endure. They are humiliations that are calculated to bring him closer to God. Few have opened themselves to God for this depth of dealing in that inner place, where something can be built up of a sweet savor. Most of us protect ourselves from the suffering and pain of the cross, and therefore, our whole life is lived on the level of the outward and visible, rather than the inner and hidden.

Aaron and his sons laid their hands on the heads of the animals as an identification with the sacrifice. We see the same principle in the letter to the Hebrews:

> Therefore, He had to be made like His brethren in all things, so that He might

> become a <u>merciful and faithful high priest</u> in things pertaining to God, to make propitiation for the sins of the people. For since He Himself was tempted in that which He has suffered, He is able to come to the aid of those who are tempted.[8]

This corresponds exactly with Aaron and his sons laying their hands upon the animals; it is an identification with the sacrifice. The priests <u>acknowledged their own sinfu</u>lness and the sins of the nation by laying their hands on that which was being offered as a substitute for them. It is the same as Job saying, "<u>I repent in dust and ashes</u>."[9] He acknowledged his need to go down into death, and that the only place for him, before a holy God, was as a dead man.

<u>Obedience</u>

> Then he [Moses] presented the second ram, the ram of ordination, and Aaron and his sons laid their hands on the head of the ram. Moses slaughtered it and took some of its blood and put it on the lobe of Aaron's right ear, and on the thumb of his right hand and on the big toe of his right foot.[10]

"<u>Hear</u>, O <u>Israel</u>!" is the beginning of all of the commandments of God. <u>Hearing is obeying, and obeying is doing.</u> From the ear to the hand, from the

---

[8] Hebrews 2:17-18
[9] Job 42:6b
[10] Leviticus 8:22-23

hearing to the doing, there must be an unhindered response. Until God has the whole of us in every kind of act, even when it contradicts our natural disposition, then He does not yet have a priest. Blood on the toe suggests divine control over the direction of our lives. Until we are prepared to remain in those tedious and monotonous situations in which God has placed us, then the blood of consecration is not upon our toe.

How many of us predicate our decisions on our own reason and logic, but at the expense of being led by the Spirit of God? We are entirely capable of drawing reasonable conclusions about how this or that will aid in God's service, or how it will further His interests, without ever having heard from Him concerning His intentions. However, we cannot enter into the high, heavenly calling without the oil and the blood. We cannot meet its demands on the basis of our own self-life or reason. But when we have become discontent with our every attempt, and have staggered and reeled before the demands of the heavenly calling, we will come to find that to enter into this calling, we must enter *into* the High Priest Himself. This reality, of which the Levitical priesthood was a type and shadow, is set forth in the book of Hebrews. There is a higher order of priesthood, more sublime, more exalted, and more demanding; it is the order of Melchizedek.[11]

WAITING IN SILENCE

After all of these sacrifices had been made for the

---

[11] See Hebrews 7:1-2

consecration of the priests, there was yet one last thing:

> At the doorway of the tent of meeting, moreover, you shall <u>remain day and night for seven days and keep the charge of the L<small>ORD</small></u>, so that you will not die, for so I have been commanded." Thus Aaron and his sons did all the things which the L<small>ORD</small> had commanded through Moses.[12]

Contemporary church life has become adept at producing schools of discipleship to process its members in three or six months, and then send them out to change the world. There is a human itch that wants to do work for God. This kind of work can never be a work of <u>eternal consequence because it is not a pure, priestly work</u>. It is in the seven days of waiting that this corrupted work is brought to death, so we no longer rush out and "do our ministry." There must first be a season of waiting <u>of an *ultimate* kind. Seven is the number of completion.</u> One can do a lot of good things, but the ultimate things, the priestly things, the apostolic things, require waiting seven days at the door of the tent of the congregation. A lot of us have fallen short at this one place. We have allowed the cutting and shedding, but we have rushed out prematurely without first waiting for the last processes of God to take place.

In the book of Acts, we find a group of believers in Antioch who were ministering unto the Lord together. Into the midst of that, the Holy Spirit could say: "Set apart for Me Barnabbas and Saul for the work to which I have called them."[13] These men were

---

[12] Leviticus 8:35-36
[13] See Acts 13:1-4

set apart, or consecrated, in an ultimate separation unto God, and therefore would have been just as content to remain in the place of worship in Antioch as to be sent out into the service of God. They had died to any self-serving desire to be used in ministry. It was a separation from those deep and subtle elements of ✷ ambition that hide themselves in the desire to *do* for God.

When we have passed through those seven days of testing, *then* we are safe to minister in a priestly way for God, free from any consideration of the benefit for ourselves. If there is something in us that wants to be heard, then our service is not priestly. We are a generation that is so ministry-minded, so doing-oriented, that we have no concept of what it takes to prepare God's servants. God sets His premium on what we *are*, not what we do. If the *doing* does not flow from the *being*, then it is not apostolic.

Overwhelming numbers of God's people view priestly service as being a man officiating over the church service, for which they are happy to pay him a salary. Consequently, they get what they pay for in the cheap, shallow and unheavenly services, which may be scripturally correct, but are unable to transform life. The congregation is not being brought into the heavenly place. All too often, Sunday services are structured for the optimum convenience of men, sufficient to allow us enough time to enjoy a sleep-in that morning, then get the service over with as soon as we can, and still allow sufficient leisure available for the football game, or whatever our good pleasure is. We need to see modern Christianity as being more the religion of convenience than a priestly service unto

God.

In priestly waiting, every fleshly thing, every human contrivance and device, every desire to perform and win some glory for ourselves, every lazy, fearful tendency to take the easy and cheap way out, will rise to the surface. A mind battle takes place, and thoughts come to mind of the practical things that need to be done and how the time should really be more usefully employed. To patiently dismiss those thoughts, and bring our minds to a place of rest in God, free from distracting thoughts, does not come readily. Through a process of repeated experiences in waiting, we bring our thoughts into subjection to Christ, so we are not influenced by every stray thought.

All that is not of God needs to be brought to the altar, to be hacked and cut up, and the lifeblood allowed to bleed out until it dies there, a spiritual sacrifice before God. There is no mystery as to why we care so little to wait upon God. We find such spiritual "blood-letting" repugnant, and such self-revelation too embarrassing and painful. We are too offended by the requirement, too ready to deem it absurd, outdated, unloving and wasteful.

On seeing a woman smash an expensive alabaster box, the indignant disciples asked Jesus: "Why this waste?"[14] Jesus replied that they were not to bother her for she had done a good work. It was the only time in the gospels that He ever acknowledged anything done by a person as being a good work. Her work was not only good, but "wherever the gospel was going to be proclaimed in the world, that which the woman had

---

[14] See Matthew 26:6-13

done would be spoken of as a memorial to her." It was an extravagant acknowledgment of the uniqueness of what she had performed. Yet the very same act in the sight of the disciples moved them to indignation *at the waste*.

Waiting before God is an acknowledgment He deserves. True waiting does not expect any reward for waiting, because if it has strings attached, it is not priestly waiting. Waiting is only waiting when we ask nothing, desire nothing and expect nothing. We make no claims, we do not require anything. We are God's creation, and He is the Creator. *That* is the posture of true priestliness.

There are needs everywhere about us, all crying out for our attention. On hearing that Lazarus, whom Jesus loved, was sick unto death, He waited two days longer in the true service of priesthood. There was no deferring to the flesh, to sentiment, to human need or to the expectation of men, but to the Father alone. True waiting is a sweet smelling savor to the Lord, all the more when one has to suffer the reproach for it by those who say to you, "Well, what are *you* doing?"

When our "doing for God" has vestiges of desire to obtain something for ourselves, then that service is no longer priestly. Pure priestly ministry does not bring to the minister anything for himself. It is totally and exclusively *unto God*. Paul often writes, "for your sake" or, "for God's sake," but he never writes, "for Paul's sake." Paul is an example of true priestliness, and therefore he would not withhold bringing the whole purpose and counsel of God. He did not consider whether it would be approved, whether men liked it, how they would react, or even whether it was appropriate. A priest is utterly selfless, without any regard for his self-interest.

It is costly, but ultimately glorious, to wait the full seven days upon God. If God requires action or activity, then it must always flow out of the place of waiting. When waiting has become so structured into our priestly life, then the acts of which God requires will come out of the rest of God. The greatest exploits of the last days will come from those who know that rest, and who, by the wastefulness of finding time for it, make waiting on God a habitual aspect of their priestly life.

Waiting inaugurates the priestly ministry, but it is not the end of it. Can you believe that one can be waiting, even in the midst of speaking? While you are speaking, you are waiting on God for the next statement. It is a remarkable disposition of an inward kind, even while one is active. This kind of waiting is virtually unknown to modern consideration, but needs to be restored. There is a conjunction between the willingness to wait, to be unseen, unknown and unheard of, that has everything to do with the power, the glory, and the authority that is exhibited when we are called upon by God to speak. We never know when that calling will come, or even if it will come, but we have to come to a priestly place where it makes no difference.

Ambition in service, a taint that finds expression in witness and ministry, will prevent the glory of God falling in fire from heaven. Being jealous for the glory of God, and the fire from heaven, is an incentive for waiting. If our motive is only success, good messages and good services, then we will not have the stamina and incentive for that final waiting, which is the necessary death that must precede the falling of the fire. This falling may express itself in a holy hush before God, a moment of such a kind that you virtually stop breathing, but you know that God is there in power.

This is not an open invitation to become "glory seekers" to delight our carnal hearts. His glory is the testimony of Himself, which we ourselves often prohibit and preclude by our own religious and ministerial actions. Men can conduct successful religion, but only priestly ministry can bring down fire from heaven, which is the glory of God. Glory is lacking in God's house, and that glory ignites and empowers the word, and transforms doctrine and mere religious services into life-changing conviction and heavenly events.

True Blessing

After the last sacrifice, and after the last waiting, and after the last waving of the sacrifice, "Aaron lifted up his hands toward the people and blessed them."[15]

Can you imagine what those hands looked like? They were steeped and impregnated with blood, right into the fingernails and every pore. He would have looked more like a butcher than a priest. When Israel fashioned a golden calf, it was the Levites who separated themselves from the rest of the profaned Israelites, and came to Moses, thereby standing on the Lord's side. They were then required to put their

---

[15] Leviticus 9:22a

swords on, and go in and out of the camp, and every man was to slay his friend, his father and his neighbor. By this act, the priests were consecrated to God, and in fact, the word "consecrated" means "hands full of blood."

So here is Aaron lifting up his hands to bless the people. Only priests can raise holy hands above men and command blessing from heaven. Only the priest has the authority, only he has been in the presence of the Most High. The reasons why *our* attempts to bless did not actually convey a blessing is because we did not have priestly hands, and they were not priestly because they were not bloody; we intoned the right words that *speak* of blessing, but the words themselves did not actually *constitute* blessing. Our hands had not been dipped in blood. A priest is not a priest if he cannot pronounce blessing, and what is his blessing if it is only a mere verbalization without bringing the palpable blessing in fact?

In my own observation, there has hardly been a word more cheapened than the word *blessing*: "Bless you brother, bless you sister … bless the Lord." It has become a pitiful cliché by people who do not even expect that something is going to be conferred by the speaking of the word. True blessing is a priestly benediction that *performs* something of a palpable and substantive kind. It transmits something out of heaven brought into the deeps of men, and blessedness is experienced.

THE GLORY OF GOD

> And he stepped down after making the sin

> offering and the burnt offering and the peace offerings. Moses and Aaron went into the tent of meeting. When they came out and blessed the people, the glory of the LORD appeared to all the people. Then fire came out from before the LORD and consumed the burnt offering and the portions of fat on the altar; and when all the people saw it, they shouted and fell on their faces.[16]

Everything had been done according to what had been commanded, and then God *Himself* ignited the sacrifice. It is interesting that the seventh day of waiting results in the eighth day of release for ministry. The number eight represents the resurrection life and power. Seven days of complete death, then the eighth day of the power and life of God Himself.

If we have not seen *that* glory, it is because we have not fulfilled *all* that the Lord commanded us to do. If there is one distinctive that is at the heart of apostolic, it is the singular jealousy for the glory of God. To have any lesser criterion for success is to rob God's people, and fixes them at a lesser level. When the glory of God appears, then the Lord appears, for the Lord *is* His glory. His glory is not some ethereal thing, but a substantive phenomenon that can be known. We have lived so long *without* it, satisfied merely with phrases *about* it, but without any real expectation *for* it. "To Him be the glory in the church"[17] was Paul's jealous desire. Without glory in the church, it is simply not the church, because it has

---
[16] Leviticus 9:22b-24
[17] Ephesians 3:21a

failed in God's purpose for it. If glory does not come through the church, it does not come at all. And if it is not in the church, then how shall it be communicated anywhere in the world?

> And when all the people saw it, they shouted and fell on their faces.[18]

This is the result of the appearing of the glory of God to men, despite their resistance, self-will and shallowness. Your face is what you are, and everything in those people came down before God when they saw that glory. There was none of that "Amen" and "Hallelujah" stuff that punctuates our charismatic services, but a prostration that was so profound and utter that anyone who rises from that never rises in the same way in which that one went down. All of your seeing, all of your reckoning, all that you value, and all that you have been planning for are affected by that going down. You cannot again go on as before. That is what happens when you fall before the demonstration of the glory of God. The God of Moses and Aaron is still God, and if He will have a priestly people on the earth as consecrated as Aaron and his sons, then that glory will again fall.

The priests were to teach the people the difference between the profane and the sacred. How can we perform this ministry when a priestly reality is absent from our own lives? Perhaps we have neglected to ascend the holy mount or have lost all desire for transfiguration glory. Perhaps we have grown content to remain outside the tent of meeting where our religious activity has become a kind of entertainment,

---

[18] Leviticus 9:24b

technically correct, but devoid of glory, devoid of the fragrance of heaven and devoid of priestly ministry. Jesus Himself came out of the holy place with God, and so must every minister who aspires to be priestly.

If we are brash, or have a metallic ring to our voices, it is the sure evidence they we have not waited in the holy place, or even recognize that there is such a place to which God is calling us. Our voices, like our faces, are a trademark and a statement of the depth of a consistent relationship with the God of all grace. In an unmistakable way, they indicate the truth and depth of a believer's relationship with his God. Ironically, when the radiance of the glory of God does come, we who bear that glory on our faces will not even know it because we will have come to a total unself-consciousness about ourselves. The radiance of God is obtained in the place of waiting in the presence of God, by those who believe that there is such a place, and have the faith to enter it, and live and move and have their being from that place. Then the world will know the difference between the sacred and the profane.

It is so easy to grow content with comfortable, undemanding meetings without expecting anything more than that. An expectation must first be rekindled in us, an expectation that the glory of God can actually fall from heaven like fire, where men are brought down on their faces, where hands are clasped over mouths, where deep breakings issue forth. If we desire this result for the wrong reasons, wanting to see people come down in great prostration by something *we* have done, then we will never see the true glory of God. How many of us, who stand behind the pulpit, have in the back of our minds that we are the ones who are going to score a home run? How much of that is unconscious, yet nevertheless there? With such subtleties of self-will in our hearts, we thereby cheat people from experiencing God's glory. When we seek to frame a message in order to impress our audience, then that is the end of the message; it is no longer a priestly word.

AS THE PRIEST, SO ALSO THE PEOPLE

This is why we need each other. However pure our priestly desire might be, we are all capable of slipping into a desire for personal glorification. Therefore, we need to be in frequent relationship with those who will detect the first signs of sinful propensities and call it to our attention. In other words, we cannot maintain this jealousy for priestly ministry on our own. It was Aaron *and* his sons. The whole congregation of Israel was assembled to witness the consecration of Aaron and his sons, because all were intimately involved and profoundly connected. The priest was not just a religious functionary who received payment for services rendered. There was a vital link: "as the priest, so also the people."

We see in Israel's history the decline of the priesthood, the loss of its purpose, and the final horror was the way in which the Messiah of Israel was treated and finally put to death at the hands of the priestly class. We see how even that high calling can go so low. When the priests have come to that place, then the nation is also in that place. If you want to study the history of Israel, then study the history of its priesthood. When Israel's priestly class was full of zeal, and had a heavenly respect for its calling, then Israel was at its zenith. When the priests began to be seduced away, then Israel declined and ultimately collapsed.

The same could be said of the church at large today. We, too, are somewhat embarrassed and offended by the cutting and bloodshed that is inseparable from priestly ministry. We too are swept up in the culture of our day, finding the entertainment, the methods, the psychology and the wisdom of our age more enlightened and engrossing than the crude insistence on radical purging and cleansing. More than we know, we have turned away from the priestly service of sacrifice and blood. It is another way of saying that we have turned away from the cross.

We are a generation of smooth professionals, with many young men, barely into their thirties, in places of ministry and high influence, often with congregations of thousands. They are often whiz-kid successes with all the "know-how" of principles, but on those rare occasions when I glimpse them on someone's television set, my stomach is sickened. It is so much a professional performance, because the seeking of God, the blood and the waiting are unknown to ministers of this kind. Too many of our ministers are coming to resemble modern Rabbis more than biblical priests, and therefore too many of our congregations are coming to resemble amiable, religious assemblies, rather than the peculiar people of God. We are too much like the world, because our ministers are themselves the picture of worldly accomplishment. Their appearance, the way they dress, their glittery rings and hairstyles show that the world has swept in.

God has established His order for true ministry: the outer layers, passable in the world, must be stripped off; then the Word must wash our nakedness; then the priestly garments are put on, one by one, in prescribed order, linen only. If the garments were other than linen, the priests would sweat. They went up on a ramp, not on steps. They did not dare lift their leg to the next step lest any flesh be glimpsed. No flesh or human sweat were to come into God's presence, both the statements of religious, human exertion. Priestly ministry can only come out of the rest of God. When we will do the prescribed thing given by God, in an exacting obedience, by the life of God, it will not be an act of human self-exertion. One of the great ironies is that more sweat is exuded on Sundays than on any other day of the week. There is more fleshly exertion to produce successful religion than we care to acknowledge. If we were more jealous for His glory than for our own honor and reputation, we would not sweat so much. The sweating shows that there is something in it for us, that is to say, we do not want to take the risk of failing before God's people.

To be priestly is to be untainted by human fretting, human contrivance and human exertion. All of the laborious requirements—the sacrifices and sprinklings, being immersed in blood and gore from finger tips to elbows—prohibit there being anything of *themselves* left to perform something priestly. This is the heart of the mystery of priesthood. It must be performed in the power of His everlasting life, not in some makeshift pumping up of ourselves into what we think priestly ministry ought to be. God's priests are so filled with the understanding of the holiness of the things that are set before them, that they do not presume to initiate anything out of their own humanity.

THE CALL TO PRIESTHOOD

There almost seems to be a calculated campaign to drive the consciousness of priesthood from the church. We are inundated with sound and noise, multimedia displays and concerts that are aimed at the senses, which not only have to be heard, but also felt. Ironically, when a minister comes who has waited in the place of silence, we are not always happy for him. We are intimidated because we thought we had it all together. We saw ourselves as well-meaning and industrious believers, who were able to quote the scriptures, and had a firm grasp on the doctrines of the faith. Then comes a visitor from heaven, a priest of God, and we are devastated. He brings an aura, a fragrance and a spirit that challenges us and reveals us to ourselves. All of a sudden, we recognize that so much of what we had been doing and saying was earthbound and stale.

We need priests who will come and minister before men only after they have ministered to God in the holy place. We need ministry from men who have first offered up their flesh—their ambitions, their vanity, their fears and greed, and their man-pleasing messages. We need men who have a heart to endure the "wearisome" requirements of God, and who will submit to the painful dealings. We need men who are prepared to see blood spurt, and wounded flesh writhe and kick and gasp for breath. We need men who will stand steadfast and immovable, who will let death be worked in them to the end, who are willing to suffer the reproach and embarrassment of inner parts being exposed. Such men are rare. They are God's priests, who alone are qualified to wield God's sword, sanctified by blood. They alone have the disposition and utter fearlessness required to cut into the flesh of God's people, and to expose the inward hidden parts of our being, to wound flesh and let its lifeblood flow out.

THE MELCHIZEDEK PRIESTHOOD

God says of His Son: "You are a priest forever according to the order of Melchizedek."[19] There has always been an abiding priesthood that is older than the Aaronic order, which was only a shadow of the greater reality. When Abraham came back from defeating the kings of Sodom, he met a mystical figure, and gave him a tenth of all that he had. Abraham deferred to this high priest, Melchizedek, who served him bread and wine. Who this Melchizedek was is not entirely known. Was he perhaps a pre-incarnate glimpse of the Son of Man, who remains a priest forever? Abraham, great man of faith that he was, recognized the authority and superiority of the man before him.

In the same way that *apostolic* and *priesthood* are connected, so too is there a connection between *sons* and *priests*. This mysterious high priest, this Melchizedek, is not descended from the same genealogy as Aaron:

Without father, without mother, without

---

[19] Hebrews 5:6b

> genealogy, having neither beginning of days nor end of life, but made like the Son of God, he remains a priest perpetually.[20]

It is a remarkable antithesis to the Aaronic priesthood, which is exactly opposite to this. The Melchizedek order is above culture, time and nationality. It is without beginning of days or ending of life. In fact, anything earthly contradicts it. The Aaronic priesthood required genealogy, ancestry and earthly identification. On the other hand, the Melchizedek order resembles the Son of God, a priest without interruption, who abides eternally. It is a priesthood to which every believer is called, not on the basis of natural qualification, but in exact proportion as we are *beyond* time, culture and nationality, *without* mother or father or ancestry, *without* beginning of days or ending of life. It is priestly service performed in a continual flow, out from the throne of God, on the basis of the power of an endless and indestructible life.

To come into this priesthood will be a wrenching, because how will your father and mother like it? To renounce your physical identification will be like a slap in their face. You have to be cut off from those things that want to establish your identification in earthly terms. It is part of the price a believer must pay, and one that cannot be easily explained to others. "Who is My mother?" said Jesus, in reply to being told that His mother and brothers were waiting outside. By an earthly evaluation that sounds cruel, but that is because we have not entered into His priestliness, and have not understood the profound detachment that a priest must have from every fleshly connection here on

---

[20] Hebrews 7:3

earth. Ironically, we will never be a better son or daughter than when we will come to this priestly detachment, where we can put off whatever depth of sickly, soulish involvement of life there might yet be between parents and children.

In other words, we need to come to an identity beyond what we are in the earthly and natural way, which does not diffuse or eliminate male or female, Jew or Gentile. Those distinctions should not be abolished, but instead, something transcendent comes out of the union of these distinct entities that creates a "new man." It is a strange paradox of being a Jew or a Gentile, a male or female, and not annulling that obvious thing, but esteeming it as from God, who gave it for His own purposes. And yet, we should not celebrate it in a way that forms a membrane between ourselves and those who are not like us. Wherever time, culture, ethnic, earthly and temporal factors are given the pre-eminent emphasis, consciously or unconsciously, we move out of priestliness, and we forfeit, therefore, the priestly ground and the power of its life. A priest is detached from racial, ethnic and cultural lines as well as from time and place. He is not at all influenced or limited by present, contemporary culture. Standing above it, he transcends it, and therefore he is relevant everywhere and at any time.

Abraham obeyed the call of God to come out of Ur of the Chaldees only *after* his father died. There was a delay in the city of Haran, where he did not hearken fully to the call of God, which was to get out of nation, kindred and father's house, and to follow the Lord into the land that was to be shown him. He collected much substance and many souls in Haran, but it was not the place of blessedness. How many of us are in the equivalent of Haran today? How many have misconstrued increase of substance and goods as if it were a sign of blessedness? More likely, we are in a place of delay, still attached to flesh, still attached to kindred and father's house, and we have not come out to begin the priestly walk where true blessedness begins.

If you want to operate from that lesser place, you can, but it will not be priestly. You come into this calling because you have come into the Son, who is the King of Righteousness as well as the King of Peace, the High Priest of God. If you are *in* the Son of Man by virtue of joining Him in His death by the power of the cross, through baptism, you are also with Him abiding as a priest continually. You are in the Melchizedek priesthood in exact proportion as you are abiding in the Son, no more and no less. It has nothing to do with natural factors, but only with resurrection life, a life offered in sacrifice and raised up in glory. We are brought to a transcendent place of identification with Him by which every natural, racial, religious, ethnic and other distinction is transcended.

> And this is clearer still, if another priest arises according to the likeness of Melchizedek, who has become such not on the basis of a law of physical requirement, but according to the power of an indestructible life.[21]

It is the same life, bursting forth out of death in resplendent glory, and now available to everyone who will give it opportunity to be expressed, but only on the condition of their own death. It is the foundation of the royal priesthood and the community of God. This kind of priesthood needs also to have as its foundation and source the endless and indestructible life of the Son. We are not going to play at being priests by building on the strength of our own expertise, ability, knowledge, religious cleverness, and even our own well-wishing intentions. The Melchizedek priesthood is based on the inheritance that has come by the blood of the Lamb, to those who have entered into the life of that blood by putting aside their own life.

The issue of resurrection is going to be one of the fiercest end-time issues for the people of God. It is going to be the plumb line of God that separates the false church from the true remnant. The false church will applaud the *doctrine* of the resurrection; but they will refuse to live in it, and by it. There has always been a great divide between those who have mere verbal profession, and those who are in that life.

SEATED IN HEAVEN

> Now if He were on earth, He would not be a priest at all.[22]

He is in another dimension, the heavenly place, and anything less would invalidate true priestliness. If we dwell on the earth, which is to say, if our values and mind-set are earthly, then we would not be priests at all. God intended that those made in His image would live in the reality of heaven, even while residing

---

[22] Hebrews 8:4a

on the earth. They are *on* it but they do not dwell *in* it. When the smoke clears at the end of the age, in the eschatological climax, there will only be two species of mankind to be found on earth: either those who dwell *in* the earth, whose hearts fail them for fear of the things that shall be coming upon the earth; or those who dwell in heaven. The one group has its values established in the earth; they are earthlings, and that is all they know, look for and expect. The other group may be living on the earth, but it is not their place of habitation. Earth is not where they reside, but the place where they serve. Are we earthlings, moored in the earth, so bound by its gravitational tug, so connected by soulish ties of affection and investment in the earth? It will take a wrench of soul before we can ascend into the heavenly place.

THE HOLY OF HOLIES

We know that both the Tabernacle in the wilderness and the Temple that came later had the same essential architectural pattern. We are given a description of the extraordinary details that went into the building of the structure. There was an outer court, which was open to the daylight without any covering. At its entrance, there was a bronze altar for sacrifice and the basin for washing, symbolic of our entry into the house of God, through the atonement of the blood of the Lamb. Proceeding further, one passed through a veil into the inner court that was covered from the elements. Only those priests whose function it was to light the holy altar of incense and to place the shewbread on the table of the Lord went into this second court. It was a room that was shut off from natural daylight, receiving its illumination from a seven-branched candlestick, a light that was not subject to the variables of the natural elements of weather and sunlight. But there was yet a final and ultimate place. It is the holiest place of all, the Holy of Holies, and there is no daily traffic there. Only the High Priest could enter that place, once a year, and only then on the basis of the blood of a pure sacrifice. There was no seven-branched candlestick, and yet it was the brightest and most glorious light of all. It was the Shekinah glory of God Himself. It was His Presence, above the mercy seat and over the ark of the Law:

> There I will meet with you; and from above the mercy seat, from between the two cherubim which are upon the ark of the testimony, I will speak to you about all that I will give you in commandment for the sons of Israel.[23]

Perhaps some of us are already emitting a groan as we become increasingly conscious of the magnitude of what this *apostolic* and *priestly* calling is. How do we move from an institutional age toward the restoration of apostolic glory in the church? How do we communicate the dimension of things that have been lost in our modern church experience? How are we to restore the sense of urgency and imminence of the things that shall shortly come to pass? How shall we warn our generation that God has appointed a day in which He will judge all nations by Him whom He has raised from the dead? How are we to be fitted for such

---

[23] Exodus 25:22

apostolic confrontation? Where do we find our courage, boldness, understanding and sensitivity? Where are we to find our answers?

> There I will meet with you; and ... speak to you about all that I will give you in commandment for the sons of Israel.[24]

This is the alternative to becoming mere technicians and adopting yet another brittle phraseology. God bids us come into the holiest place of all, the high-priestly place, open to those who come in the form of the Son of God, without father or mother, or beginning or ending of days. It is the source of the indestructible life, a source of inspiration and anointing, of words that He will give us, if indeed we desire to fulfill the mandate of God.

There is an entry within that veil, by the Holy Spirit, symbolized by the burning incense on the altar that continually ascends up to God. Within the veil, there is a seeing in a much different light. It is a deeper place where the serious and purposeful things of God are made known to the believer. We will never glimpse the truth of God as He is, except in *this* light. We will never fulfill the apostolic mandate except it be by the words that are given in this place.

WITHIN THE VEIL

I had waited a long time for such an entry. As much as I am at war with the secular world, something of its concept of evolution yet lingered with me, so that I thought that I had to "evolve" into a higher spiritual

---

[24] Ibid., v.22

state, by which I would then be able to enter into this holiest place. However, I stumbled upon a series of teachings that were entitled, "Within the Veil," and something in my inner man went *click*. I began to play the first message with a sense of anticipation, but as soon as I heard the first few statements, I was tempted to shut the machine off. Some "hillbilly" American was speaking, whose speech was coarse and ungrammatical, not my style at all, but as my finger went to the stop button, I hesitated, because something now began to reach me beyond his accent. He was coming from a place beyond nationality, beyond culture, beyond time, beyond father or mother or beginning or ending of days. I continued to listen, tape by tape, of a man whose frustration was much like my own. He had the same risings and fallings of the spiritual life, the good days and the bad days. As I followed him through the letter to the Hebrews, he showed that the Law was only a shadow of the good things to come, rather than the very form of those things, and that it could not make perfect those who draw near. He went on to explain that there was One who came in point of time who could. His blood was better than the blood of bulls and of goats and of sacrifices. He had entered by His own blood into the heavenly place, and entered once and for all.

In all of our impressive spiritual sophistication, we have not allowed these words to impact upon our souls. Jesus bids us to enter also, and to enter boldly, not on the basis of our natural qualification, but by His blood. We have come to think of His blood only in terms of our atonement, and indeed it is sufficient to wash away sin and guilt, but His blood has done something more; it has opened a new and living way.

I remember the night I heard the last tape. I was in bed, my Bible open, and listening as he described how he came to a Sunday morning service as a minister, weary and defeated, in that kind of terrible <u>monotony and predictability which our churches can so</u> easily become. But there was a woman that morning in the service who was a very <u>bright light</u>. She could hardly contain herself. She kept waving her arm in the air, wanting to give a testimony.

"Yes, sister," he said. And she replied,

"I just want to say that I have entered within the holiest place of all." He was quick to correct her,

"You mean to say that you hope to enter." (After all she was only a housewife, he thought.)

"No," she said, "I have entered."

"By what means?" he said.

"<u>By faith in the blood of Jesus, and the veil that</u> was rent by His flesh! I simply drew near with a true heart of faith, and I confessed that I do enter right now into the holiest place of all," she replied.

She said that something had happened to her, and that she had entered into a "new place." And the evidence of that was clearly visible on her face. Before that service had ended, one by one, people were getting up in the congregation and making a <u>simple confession of their "entering right now" on</u> the basis of the blood of Jesus into a new and living way. The pastor himself entered, for which reason I was now hearing his tapes. He experienced a new kind of <u>enablement, an enhanced and deepened quality of apostolic faith.</u> He received a fresh source of creativity and originality from a place of communion with God in the holiest place of all.

At about this point I shut off my tape machine. I took my glasses off and thought for a moment, reflecting upon my years in Christ—all the frustration, the rising and the falling; and I just simply breathed a prayer, flat on my back. I said, "Lord, right now, not on the basis of any qualification, I do enter into the holiest place of all by the blood of Jesus and the veil rent by His flesh. Amen." I believe I have been in that place ever since, holding fast the confession of the faith.

A new kind of freedom from the torment of wrestling with flesh commenced. Something dealt with my flesh when I entered in through the veil of His torn flesh, in a way I can hardly understand or communicate. Every power of Hell will seek to steal this from us with suggestions like: "Oh, this is only a play on words, just a kind of biblical rhetoric. There is no real, actual place of entry. This heavenly thing is only a vapor, an intangible thing. You have all that you need by virtue of your new birth. This is only a conceit on your part. Look, you are still the same!" That is why we are encouraged to hold fast the confession of our faith.

> Therefore let us draw near with confidence to the throne of grace, so that we may receive mercy and find grace to help in time of need.[25]

If we shall not receive mercy and find grace, then how shall we give it? We are therefore bidden to

Heb 4:1

enter. It is the Sabbath rest that God has prepared for His people. Religious acts and works that stem from a bad conscience, that is to say, something that you feel obliged to do, are called *dead works* by God. The work of God comes always and eminently out of the rest of God, and is always performed on the "Sabbath" day. It alone is that act which brings sight to the blind. When the Jews of Jesus' time were antagonized and stupefied at this bewildering Man who performed these glorious things on the wrong day, He could say to them in utter simplicity that it was the Father who was doing the works. You will know when you are in the rest of God when there is a deep-seated peace in your inner being. This does not mean there will be an absence of trial or tension, but in the midst of the turmoil of it, you are in the Shekinah place, the holiest place of all, independent of the circumstances that are flurrying everywhere about you.

We can understand Paul better when he says that he lives and moves and has his being in Him. Where are we and where do we desire to be, and where have we the faith to be? Do we desire an apostolic participation in the eternal purposes of God? For those who do, there is a high-priestly place available for us as a life that flows, and which is indestructible. Faith comes by hearing, and hearing by the word of God. This is not some fanciful play on words, but something to be earnestly considered. Faith is now, and the hour has struck and the time is short, and God is requiring a fulfillment that can only come from this place within the veil. Have the faith to enter with a true and sincere heart in full assurance of faith.

SAVED TO THE UTTERMOST!

The priestliness we are called to is union with the High Priest. We become one with Him, which means that everything in us will need to be sanctified, every aspect of our life, even the most mundane. In fact, it is in the most mundane places that the truth of sanctification is the most precious. The most ordinary things become holy. The whole of life becomes a sacrament. Eating is no longer a gastronomic activity. We dare not approach our bedrooms, our kitchens, our chance conversations without feeling that sanctifying influence of this High Priest within us. There is no longer trivial or careless talk. Everything is significant, consecrated, having an eternal weight of glory. It is a transfiguration of life itself by bringing into it a heavenly dimension.

Priesthood is not a physical heritage like that of Aaron's, but rather a spiritual heritage by virtue of entering *into* resurrection life. To do less, and to minister out of anything other than the resurrection life, is to fall short of priestly ministry. The burdens and demands that inhere in this priesthood are far greater than the Levitical priesthood, but the power to meet and to fulfill them is likewise greater. To put this garment on is to put on resurrection life. We have heard good messages, good teachings and good ministry, but there is a difference between that which is good and that which is empowered by a "life out of death" reality. Without death there is no resurrection life. Without entering into death, there is no entering into the life and calling of the High Priest.

It is better that we remain insensitive and

unmoved, and be willing to wait for those burdens of God that come as ex<u>pressions out of the indestructible life from heaven</u>, rather than fashion burdens for ourselves out of guilt, or our own ideas of what is appropriate and spiritual. Such self-wrought and convenient burdens will burst like a bubble when the first challenge to sacrifice self-interest touches them. The burdens must come from the indestructible, resurrection life of the King of Righteousness in heaven. They must come from the life of the True Priest, who neither has, nor desires, any earthly inheritance, who is not bound to earth and upon whom nothing of this world has a grip and a hold. When we put on this priestly garment, fastened on with cords that ascend to heaven, we are bound to heavenly realities, leaving behind the constraints of this earth.

<u>Jesus is a priest forever</u> according to the order of *Heb 5* Melchizedek. He is able, therefore, to save to the uttermost, completely, perfectly and eternally all those who draw near to God through Him. We need more of this kind of salvation and far less of the shabby kind that produces countless tens of thousands who are called "saved" but who are not <u>consecrated or converted</u>.[26] If our lives are one long struggle to hang on until the end to find at least a little niche in heaven, we have surely not been brought to salvation by a Melchizedek priest, because one brought to God through Him is saved *to the uttermost*!

We need more of this "uttermost" salvation and less pre-packaged evangelistic techniques. We need more priests bringing the conviction and mercy of God down from His throne in heaven, and less well-

---

[26] See chapter on Apostolic Conversion

meaning men bringing their own devices and systems forth out from their own heads. We need to stop appealing to men on the basis of all the benefits that will accrue to them if they would only "accept" Jesus. A true priest would gag and choke on such terminology and egocentric appeals that are based on benefits to self; he would be repulsed by that kind of appeal because it is a contradiction in terms. It is *not* salvation in the biblical sense of the word. True <u>salvation is to be saved *out* of oneself, and to be saved out of oneself is to be saved *to the uttermost*</u>.

How can we bring men to true salvation when we ourselves have not been truly converted, when we ourselves are still bound in self-interest, when we have not experienced the exchange of our old fleshly life for the resurrection life? God's Holy Seed is meant to reproduce after its own kind, but all around us we see reproduced the image of ourselves, our incompleteness and carnality. Everywhere about us mankind is perishing, even while they are living, and therefore we desperately need more priests to be the instruments of the salvation of men on the basis of the power of the indestructible life.

SUMMARY

The final outworking of the mystery of Israel and the church[27] at the end of the age will be the natural sons of Abraham (the Jews) meeting, as the Abraham of old, the priestly people of God, those who can confer blessing, those who radiate heaven. That meeting will reveal the God of this priestly remnant. This final ministry to Israel will be the moving of them to jealousy. What a staggering thing for a Jew to find in a Gentile the very priestliness to which they were called as a priestly nation! If that will not move them to jealousy as it radiates out of Gentile faces, then there is no other salvation for them. They need to encounter what Abraham encountered thousands of years ago, and when he saw it, he instantly recognized Melchizedek as the priest of the Most High God. He paid tithes to Melchizedek, though he was to become the father of nations, as Israel is to become. Abraham still had to find in that encounter a priest whose qualification and knowledge of heaven exceeded his own. This is how it will end for the remnant church, called to live and move in this reality.

CHAPTER 2

Apostolic Perception - Eternity

> Therefore we do not lose heart, but though our outer man is decaying, yet our inner man is being renewed day by day. For momentary, light affliction is producing for us an eternal weight of glory far beyond all comparison, while we look not at the things which are seen, but at the things which are not seen; for the things which are seen are temporal, but the things which are not seen are eternal.[1]

There is a danger that we will dismiss these verses as biblical rhetoric, a kind of fanciful manner of speaking peculiar to Paul, nodding in agreement that it has a nice ring to it, but completely lose what is being said.

---

[1] 2 Corinthians 4:16-18

However, the foundation of the apostolic mindset is the true apprehension of eternity, not only as anticipation of a future enjoyment, but of a present appropriation. This is what makes the church a peculiar entity in the earth. To lose the meaning of eternity is to lose everything, and we will be condemned to being mundane and ordinary, institutional and mechanical, a dull predictability rather than a joyous reality. The apostle Paul lived and moved and had his being in the eternal dimension, and yet, that did not condemn him to irrelevancy. On the contrary, it made him all the more relevant, and so will it make us also.

In the scriptures just quoted, we find two references to the word *eternal*. Eternity had become so powerfully real to Paul that it had practical consequences for his living: He was a man who had been shipwrecked, beaten with rods, left for dead, stoned, reviled, persecuted and defamed, yet he could truthfully reckon those things as being momentary, light afflictions. Either Paul had tossed every reasonable criterion and rationality to the wind, or he had a standard of which we know very little. Paul saw redemptive suffering in this lifetime as being merely *momentary* and *light*.

Paul did not dwell on his sufferings in some kind of morbid way. He had caught a glimpse of the eternal weight of glory that would be his reward, but only to the degree he willingly and joyfully submitted to the circumstances that his obedience occasioned. The fact that *we* have not yet experienced a measure of comparable suffering indicates that we have been exercising some lesser obedience, if it is obedience at all, which has not excited the world's hatred against us.

If we do not see the eternal weight of glory in similar measure to Paul, then light affliction will seem for us to be very burdensome. Everything depends on our actual knowing of the eternal realm. We may know that eternity is there, and distant, and something that we will obtain after this life, but we have not brought the eternal dimension into the present in a way that actually affects our manner and conduct.

SEEING THE UNSEEN

Looking upon and being engaged with the things that are eternal, unseen and invisible are God's provision for bearing the persecution that must come in this life. Everything in the world conspires against eternity. The world clamors for the attention of our senses, wanting to fill our eyes with all of its voluptuous images. It seeks to keep us looking *down*. The things that are *seen* give us assurance and confidence, and it will take an apostolic determination to close out the things that are visible, and to focus and dwell upon the things that are invisible and eternal. Such a focus will produce in us a growing indifference to the things that are of the world, those visible and sensual things that are a gratification for our soulish, physical life. Do we see this world as under judgment? Do we see its values and systems as soon to pass away? Or are we overwhelmed and intimidated by the things that are visible?

> Therefore if you have been raised up with Christ, keep seeking the things above, where Christ is, seated at the right hand of

> God. Set your mind on the things above, not on the things that are on earth. For you have died and your life is hidden with Christ in God. When Christ, who is our life, is revealed, then you also will be revealed with Him in glory.[2]

We may "believe" in eternity, but to what extent have we actually agreed with the world that eternity is not relevant until *after* this life? Eternity is not merely a time frame that is endless; it is profoundly and foremost a qualitative thing that is available now. When we begin to see all our moments set in the context of eternity, we will bring to those moments a seriousness that we would not otherwise have had. God has called the church to the apostolic task of bringing eternity into time, of bringing the reality of heaven down into this earth.

The book of Revelation begins by John writing of the things that shall shortly come to pass. There is an urgency in his apostolic writing, and yet it is almost two thousand years later, and these things have not happened. John was writing and speaking from a mindset that God intends to be characteristic of believers in *every* generation. The true sense of eternity will bring into our whole being a new dynamic of urgency about the events that are imminent: the appearing of the Lord, the establishing of His millennial Kingdom and the apocalyptic[3] conclusion of the ages.

Other than as technically correct doctrine, few of

---

[2] Colossians 3:1-4
[3] *Apocalyptic* means the breaking in of God into time and history in judgment.

us have impressed the world or communicated to it the truth of what lies beyond death. How can we if we are not ourselves presently in that dimension? We know that the whole world lies in the power of the evil one, the father of lies. Lying is everywhere about us; it is in the very air that we breathe, and one of the greatest lies is the renunciation and rejection of eternity. Men are living their lives as if *this* life is the total purpose for being. By only assenting to the doctrine of eternity as the reality that comes to us *after* death, we have given ourselves over to the same lie. We are only in the truth of God when our very existence, presence and character refute the lie.

We need to come to the world as people who bring the eternal dimension into our daily, ordinary considerations. When we do, those things no longer become mundane; everything becomes charged with eternity. If we stand before an audience, it becomes more than delivering a correct message. We ought to sense that the consequences of what we communicate are momentous—even life or death for the hearer. Everything is charged with a meaning beyond what one can define. Eternity has been brought into the *now*, and God is being revealed from the dimension in which He dwells.

AN APOSTOLIC DISTINCTIVE

Wherever we find ourselves in any given culture or society, how affected or impressed are we by what is visible before us? When Paul said he was a citizen of heaven, it was not an accidental, cheap phrase, but a statement of fact. Paul had his effectual being in heaven, and to be apostolic is to be heavenly—nothing more and nothing less.

> For we know that if the earthly tent which is our house is torn down, we have a building from God, a house not made with hands, eternal in the heavens. For indeed in this house we groan, longing to be clothed with our dwelling from heaven.[4]

Apostolic "knowing" is something that is registered in our inner man by which we long and groan. Do we feel the weight of our mortality, and yearn to be freed of this tent, and to come into what shall be the ultimate thing given by God by which we shall be eternally clothed? Right now, so long as we must endure our mortal bodies, we endure them with groans. How different from those of us who pamper and perfume our bodies, who adorn ourselves with the latest fashions and fads. Our body is just a necessary contrivance and convenience that houses our spirit. Like Paul, I am not disparaging the body, but there is something that is expressed here as a longing and groaning that is at the heart of apostolic. It can only be expressed by one who has crossed into the eternal realm, and who *knows* it. We are too much at home in the body, too much body-conscious, focused on how we appear, how we clothe it, how we feed it, how it looks, and do not realize to what degree body-consciousness robs us from coming into a true reality in God.

The whole world insists we conform to its values, and as long our mindset is essentially in the temporal

---

[4] 2 Corinthians 5:1-2

and earthly realm, we shall be the world's victims. If we only gaze at the things that are seen, and do not fix our eyes on the things that are invisible and eternal, we will be swept into the world. No one will ever fault us, but it will rob us of a consciousness of God in the eternal realm.

STRANGERS IN THE WORLD

To live, move and have our being in eternity will make us strange and peculiar to all those who are outside of that reality. We will increasingly find ourselves pilgrims and sojourners in the world, looking for a city not made with hands. We are those who are always looking for something that is not in view, but our very anticipation of it actually has an influence in bringing those things to pass:

> Since all these things are to be destroyed in this way, what sort of people ought you to be in holy conduct and godliness, looking for and hastening the coming of the day of God, because of which the heavens will be destroyed by burning, and the elements will melt with intense heat![5]

According to this verse, there is a suggestion that the "day of God" or the "day of the Lord's appearing" is not a fixed date. In other words, it will not take place independent of the condition of those who make up the believers in every generation. In fact, it is *our very condition* that releases the Lord to return to this earth. We can actually hasten the day of the Lord's

---
[5] 2 Peter 3:11-12

appearing by being the kind of people we ought to be. To come into the eternal realm, then, becomes for us the issue of the Lord's coming to establish His kingdom.

When Paul spoke to Greek philosophers on Mars Hill about a God who has appointed a day in which He shall judge all nations by Him whom He has raised from the dead,[6] it was as natural to him as breathing. He was not at all embarrassed to step from philosophy to theology in the same breath. For Paul it was not a matter of going from the secular to the sacred; it was *all* sacred, all eternal, all heavenly and all real. Paul dwelt in this eternal dimension, and brought it to bear on all of his earthly considerations. Eternity is the issue of heaven or hell, and we are going to be remarkably ill-equipped to speak of either unless the consciousness of eternity affects our every waking hour.

The whole world lies in massive deception, completely mindless with regard to the issue of eternity. It is a category that has no meaning for them. Paul's message to the philosophers of Greece was that the whole purpose of human existence is to seek after God that we might find Him. Though it sounds so embarrassing, so simplistic and intellectually dull to the mindset of philosophical man, it nevertheless stands as God's very purpose for all of our being.

Why do we not speak with that same simplicity, that same urgency and that same absoluteness? Mankind will accuse us of being dogmatic, narrow-minded and intolerant, and for that reason, many of us

---

[6] See Acts 17:30-31

are intimidated into silence. Paul was not intimidated; he burned with the reality of eternity, and took every opportunity to express the truth of God to those in the world who were bound by its values and mindset.

Absoluteness is the height of offense to a world that is relativistic and pluralistic. They do not want to be told that there is anything that is absolute, that there are only two eternal alternatives. However, they need to be told, not only by a people who bring the correct doctrines, but by those who come with the burning conviction of what they say. Do we really believe God has fixed a day in which He will judge the world in righteousness? Our apostolic task is to bring an unwanted and unwelcome message to an indifferent world, and it is a message we can only bring in the same proportion that we can demonstrate it. It is not enough to be "correct"; we have to come to mankind, as it were, *from* the eternal place.

ETERNITY AND RESURRECTION LIFE

Paul wrote to Timothy:
> Fight the good fight of faith; take hold of the eternal life to which you were called.[7]

It is evident that Paul is not speaking of some future time, but *now*! Eternal life is a dimension that co-exists with time and needs to be constantly contended for. Contending for the faith that was once given to the saints is more than just a command to embrace their doctrines, but an invitation to come into a certain dimension of being. It is not going to make

---

[7] 1 Timothy 6:12a

you other-worldly and irrelevant; you are not going to become dreamy or visionary. Rather, it is an abiding in the God who inhabits eternity. If we secretly covet the world's admiration, if we want to succeed on the world's terms, if we want to find ways to be polite and to address our Christian convictions in a manner by which the world can receive them, then we have lost or have never had an apostolic view of the faith or eternity.

On Mars Hill, Paul confronted the men of Athens:

> He [God] has fixed a day in which He will judge the world in righteousness through a man whom He has appointed, having furnished proof to all men by raising Him from the dead.[8]

The proof of the resurrection was the presence of Paul before them. Paul not only proclaimed the doctrine of resurrection and judgment, he was himself a demonstration of that same resurrection life. Paul lived in the power of the age to come, and when anyone stands before men and speaks to them penetratingly out of that life, then God has furnished proof to those men.

There is a real entry into the eternal dimension through the reality of resurrection life. Mere *approval* of doctrine is not enough; we need to live and move and have our being in Jesus Christ, or our words about an imminent judgment will be without conviction. Do we really want to see all men everywhere repent? If so, they need to see eternity already in us, and they will be eternally condemned unless they receive Him in

---

[8] Acts 17:31

whose name we come.

We are moving towards a final and ultimate confrontation with the spirit of the world. Something timeless and eternal must be presented to men by those who have already laid hold of eternal life, who are not just awaiting some future state. They are already appropriating it, and bringing it into their present consideration. Something must come again into the atmosphere of God's corporate people, a sense of urgency, a sense of imminence and of the things that will shortly come to pass. The rejection, the reproach and the persecution, which will come to us for bearing an unwelcome word to mankind, needs to be only a momentary and light affliction.

True Biblical Faith

The giants of the faith of Hebrews 11 were all eternity-minded; they were foundationally rooted in an overcoming faith:

> Now faith is the assurance of things hoped for, the conviction of things not seen. For by it the men of old gained approval. By faith we understand that the worlds were prepared by the word of God, so that what is seen was not made out of things which are visible. By faith Abel offered to God a better sacrifice than Cain, through which he obtained the testimony that he was righteous, God testifying about his gifts, and through faith, though he is dead, he still speaks. By faith Enoch was taken up so that he would not see death; AND HE WAS NOT

FOUND BECAUSE GOD TOOK HIM UP; for he obtained the witness that before his being taken up he was pleasing to God. And without faith it is impossible to please Him, for he who comes to God must believe that He is, and that He is a rewarder of those who seek Him.[9]

The reward God offers is essentially not in *this* life, but in the life to come. True faith is a faith that does not expect its reward in *this* life, but *afterwards*. The men of old gained approval by their faith, but they did not obtain the promise:

> By faith Abraham, when he was called to go out into a place which he should *after* receive for an inheritance, obeyed; and he went out, not knowing whither he went.[10]

The word *after* is a critical and key word in the definition of biblical faith. Biblical faith does not expect or look for its reward, answer, consummation, fulfillment or gratification *now*, but *after*. This is totally contrary to the tenor and spirit of the world which looks for gratification *now*.

There is a conflict of two wisdoms, one is based on immediate gratification *now*, and the other is predicated upon what comes *after*. Everything that is natural, soulish and carnal expects, deserves and wants its gratification *now*. That is why we need to be weaned from natural gratification, and to find our orientation and being in a reality beyond this life, in a heavenly citizenship. Mankind would rather predicate

---

[9] Hebrews 11:1-6
[10] Ibid., v.8 King James Version of the Bible. Emphasis mine.

its life on *reason* rather than on faith. Faith is unseen, but man wants to see, to be instantly gratified; man wants *now*.

Abraham, the great father of faith, was not only called to go *out*, but also called to go *into* a place he was to receive *after* for an inheritance. The words "inheritance" and "heir" convey a theme that is repeated throughout both the Old and New Testament scriptures. Inheritance implies something that comes *after*, usually after a death.

> By faith he lived as an alien in the land of promise, as in a foreign land, dwelling in tents with Isaac and Jacob, fellow heirs of the same promise.[11]

This is the foundation of Abrahamic faith. Isaac, Jacob and the saints of old had the same foundation: they had the immovable confidence that they would be the heirs of promise, predicated on what was spoken by God.

"All these died in faith, without receiving the promises."[12] The promises were *not* to be realized in their own lifetimes. They all died, without exception, *not* having received the promises. Not one of them received the reward of their life of faith and sacrifice in this life, but there was an expectation of an inheritance *after*. They were *assured* of the reward, the promise and the inheritance. Their lives were therefore distinguished by a walk of faith as pilgrims and strangers, embracing the hope and the inheritance, though it was yet far off.

---

[11] Hebrews 11:9
[12] Ibid., v.13

Abraham was called out of Ur of the Chaldees to the land of promise, but once he was in the land, which is to say, when he was in the right place, it was strange and foreign to him. In a sense, he was uncomfortable, because it was not yet the time to inherit it. After this life, and in the resurrection of the dead, there will be an entering into the eternal fulfillment of the promise. Biblical faith, therefore, rests on the assurance of resurrection. Abraham was expecting an eternal inheritance, which is why Paul could say that if there was no resurrection for us, then we of all men are most to be pitied.

The promulgation of the faith today is a far cry from the faith of Abraham. Faith is almost invariably invoked for the here and now: "receive your healing, receive a boyfriend or girlfriend, an apartment, a job, a Cadillac, and you can receive it now if you only have the faith." The emphasis is on the payoff *now*. But for the great fathers of the faith, it was an inheritance they would receive *after*. Even though they were physically in the land of promise, it was not yet the fulfillment of the promise for them.

We are in the faith of Abraham when, like him, we are strangers and aliens, not only in the world, but also in the land of promise. We need to look for the coming of the Lord, to long for His appearing and the coming of a millennial, future and eternal fulfillment of the promise. That is why eternity needs to come into our consciousness *now*. The world says, "If you are heavenly-minded, you are of no earthly good." In fact, the opposite is true. Except you are heavenly-minded, except you are eternity-minded, you are of no earthly good. Every value that the world celebrates as right and true is a lie. What the earth needs is not more earth, but more heaven. Eternity must come into time, the holy into the profane, the sacred into the everyday by a people who are already walking in heaven as if it is the very foundation of their life and being. Now *that* is the only true faith.

Despite every appearance to the contrary, the promises of God are predicated entirely upon His honor, the truth of His word and His ability to fulfill it. Can you die with confidence believing that you will receive the promise, though you have not seen it in your lifetime? Can you believe it with such a quality of conviction that it affects not only how you live, but also how you die? The faith leaves no room for disappointment, dejectedness or sullenness. This gives us a much more realistic understanding of what the purpose for this present life is, as well as the nature of the payoff in the life to come.

THE PROMISES OF GOD

> All these died in faith, without receiving the promises, but having seen them and having welcomed them from a distance, and having confessed that they were strangers and exiles on the earth.[13]

The promises have to do with the fulfillment of specific statements God has made to the patriarchal fathers of the faith. For example, a promise was made to David that a descendant of his would rule over the house of Israel forever. The disciples who were with

---

[13] Hebrews 11:13

Jesus after His resurrection listened to Jesus speak for forty days on the things pertaining to the kingdom of God. They asked Jesus, "Lord, is it at this time You are restoring the kingdom to Israel?"[14] The kingdom has ever and always been the political rule of God in the earth; the law shall go forth out of Zion and the word of the Lord out of Jerusalem.[15] That may not mean much to us as modern believers, but it has meant a great deal to generations of Jews who lived and waited for the fulfillment of that promise.

Abraham's looking for a "city whose Builder and Maker is God" is synonymous with looking for and hastening the coming theocratic Kingdom. The issue of God's kingdom in the sense of His ruling over His creation is the issue of God's glory. It is all the more to His glory that this rule will take place in the literal land of Promise, in the capital of that Land, Jerusalem, the city of peace, on the holy hill of Zion. If we do not have this perspective when we read these verses in the book of Hebrews, our understanding will have a limited, subjective meaning, but it is not the *full* meaning.

To long for the Lord's appearing is not to be understood as an emotional palpitation of the heart. He is coming to be vindicated in the very place where He was publicly humiliated, where they put a sign up over His head in three languages, "Jesus of Nazareth, King of the Jews." In that place alone, He will establish His rule over His creation. To love God is to love Him in the sense of desiring to see the fulfillment of all that is rightly His. Abraham understood this. It

---

[14] Acts 1:6b
[15] See Isaiah 2:1-4

was the gospel that was preached to him. It contained a promise of a coming kingdom that would establish God's glory. It was to be revealed through His rule over a creation that has long rejected Him. This is the hope and the promise, for which fulfillment believers of ages past waited, but did not receive in their lifetime; they all died not having received the promises.

Can we claim to be "looking to Jesus" and wanting to be with Him, and yet not have a concern or awareness of what it will take to eternally glorify Him? That is why both things are mentioned in the same chapter: "All these died in faith, without receiving the promises, but having seen them…"[16]

Seeing "them" is plural as against seeing "Him" who is invisible, something singular. It is not the pitting of one against the other. They saw the Lord *and* His coming in the context of what His coming means; namely, the issue of His glory forever. We are moving toward the completion of history, and into the millennial and eternal realm—the things that come *after*. The saints of old could therefore endure; they both saw and desired the end. They lived in the expectation of it as a yet future fulfillment that profoundly affected how they lived here on earth. They saw the faith in its eschatological, apocalyptic and theocratic setting. This was the faith which they contended for, and for which many of them suffered the loss of their bodily lives.

"They confessed that they were strangers and pilgrims in the earth."[17] Our earthly status and tenure

---

[16] Hebrews 11:13a
[17] Ibid., v.13b

will be radically altered if we really embrace this view. It is an inevitable consequence. Being a stranger and a pilgrim suggests that one will be uncomfortable in the world, even chafed by its values and premises. It means you can never succeed in it, or be at home in it because you will always be looking for something beyond and other. It is a prickly feeling to be strange, to not belong, because everything in modern society seeks to make you feel accepted and approved. But to feel odd and strange, and never able to fit in comfortably, is something that is not gratifying for the flesh.

It may well be that the whole carnal character of the church, and the tremendous fall-out rate, has something to do with the kind of message that people are hearing from their inception in the things of God. It is not centered in an eternal view of the kind that believers of old had.

Have you noticed how a minister is called in to initiate the sessions of Congress by opening in prayer? Or the inauguration of a new President? It is an alliance between the world and the church by which the church sanctifies and endorses this present world. We do not challenge its assumptions, nor bring to the attention of the world that its time is limited, that God has established a day in which He will judge all men. We fail to tell them that this world is under judgment, and that God is not slack concerning His promise, that the day of the Lord *will* come, that He is not willing that any should perish. If we do not voice that message, and instead condescend to bring a "religious" veneer to the secular world, we reinforce the world in its lies. We allow them to go on without any consciousness of eternity or the eternal issues of heaven and hell. We ourselves are not that persuaded of heaven, and therefore we are not able to persuade men of hell. If eternity is only a category rather than a passionate conviction, then we have no message for the world. And if the church is not evangelistic in the apostolic sense, then is it the church? One of the principal functions of the church is to proclaim the gospel of the coming kingdom, including the message of soon-coming judgment.

OUR TRUE DWELLING PLACE

When God gathers up His elect, He will gather them up "from the four corners of heaven." That does not mean we are going to be in another stratosphere. Both His elect and the unbelievers will be situated on *terra firma*, but both will be *dwelling* in two radically and diametrically opposed places. One will dwell *in* the earth, they will look *down* for their gratification. The others are those who dwell *in* heaven while they are yet *on* the earth. They are looking for the city whose builder is God. Their eye is suffused with the things that are unseen and eternal.

Jesus had a conversation once with a ruler of the Jews, a man named Nicodemus, who was the epitome of Jewish religious ethics. If there was no God, then what Nicodemus represented was the perfect answer for human ideals. But he sensed something about Jesus that exploded all of his religious categories. And though he could not understand Him, he was probing to find out, lest he missed it:

"Rabbi, we know that You have come from

> God as a teacher; for no one can do these signs that You do unless God is with him."[18]

It was the earthly man asking earthly questions, but he received a heavenly answer from a heavenly Man:

> "No one has ascended into heaven, but He who descended from heaven, even the Son of Man [alternate translations add "who is in heaven"]. [19]

Jesus let Nicodemus know that though they may be physically in Jerusalem, He was Himself *in heaven*. Does that bewilder us? How can anyone be standing in Jerusalem, and say that He is in heaven? If we do not yet understand the seeming contradiction, we have not yet attained to a faith that will allow us to endure.

True faith takes the ordinary and mundane and brings to it the quality of eternity. True faith brings eternity into time. Mankind was created in God's image to live in the eternal dimension. We were created to live in righteousness, truth, love and reality, but the world is so removed from God that it has become stunted; it thinks that everything of consequence is in this present world. It is a contorted and restricted living that is not a true living at all. The ministry of the church is to demonstrate the message of a kingdom that is at hand: "Look, here it is! Look at the reality. Look at us. We are a people who are free from intimidation, fear, anxiety and distress!"

---

[18] John 3:2b
[19] John 3:13

The Afflictions of the Saints

Paul saw the eternal weight of glory that made his present afflictions both momentary and light. It is a seeing that affects the present in a very tangible and substantial way. It is a provision of God to keep us from becoming cowards. There are believers in times past who actually went with rejoicing to the stake to be burned alive. They saw martyrdom as the logic and endorsement of the truth of their faith. They were assured of the crown, already rejoicing in the anticipation of the reward, so much so that they hardly felt the flames burn them up.

The eternal weight of glory, the eternal reward, is ours in the measure of our willingness to enter into the sufferings of Christ. Redemptive sufferings precede the glory, and the glory will be ours to the degree that we bear the sufferings. If we intend to come into the apostolic context of the faith, we will be making ourselves candidates for suffering in one form or another. We will be a marked people before the principalities and powers of the air. If the Devil inflicts suffering upon the saints because they are entertaining apostolic and eternal things, then the greater the character that is shaped and worked by the bearing of it. The patience and long-suffering that are wrought in us are only possible because of the "joy that is set before us."

The Eternal Mindset

And indeed if they had been thinking of

> that country from which they went out, they would have had opportunity to return.[20]

This means not only the country, but also the values of the country and the things that are celebrated in this present world.

> But as it is, they desire a better country, that is, a heavenly one. Therefore God is not ashamed to be called their God; for He has prepared a city for them.[21]

We are chastened in *this* life as preparation for the life *to come*:

> Furthermore, we had earthly fathers to discipline us, and we respected them; shall we not much rather be subject to the Father of spirits, and live? For they disciplined us for a short time as seemed best to them, but He disciplines us for our good, so that we may share His holiness. All discipline for the moment seems not to be joyful, but sorrowful; yet to those who have been trained by it, *afterwards* it yields the peaceful fruit of righteousness.[22]

Notice the practical implication *now* because you believe in the *afterwards*:

> Therefore, strengthen the hands that are weak and the knees that are feeble, and make straight paths for your feet So that the limb which is lame may not be put out of joint, but rather be healed. Pursue peace

---

[20] Hebrews 11:15
[21] Hebrews 11:16
[22] Hebrews 12:9-11. Emphasis mine.

> with all men, and the sanctification without which no one will see the Lord. See to it that no one comes short of the grace of God; that no root of bitterness springing up causes trouble, and by it many be defiled; that there be no immoral or godless person like Esau, who sold his own birthright for a single meal. For you know that even afterwards, when he desired to inherit the blessing, he was rejected, for he found no place for repentance, though he sought for it with tears.[23]

The intention of the Holy Spirit in these words is entirely eschatological. The whole gist and meaning, using Esau as an example, is to bring us into the awareness that this life's preparation is for the eternal, and that *this* is the inheritance that comes *after*. Esau was unable to deny himself a meal. He was so rooted in immediate gratification that he could not hold for a later time the gratification that he had to have now.

The whole purpose of discipline or chastisement, which is to say, the painful dealings of God against our flesh, is to break the power of the need to be gratified now. The definition of a son is one who can defer his gratification for the reward that comes *after*.

> But remember the former days, when, after being enlightened, you endured a great conflict of sufferings, partly by being made a public spectacle through reproaches and tribulations, and partly by becoming sharers with those who were so treated. For you

---

[23] Ibid., vv.12-17

> showed sympathy to the prisoners and accepted joyfully the seizure of your property, knowing that you have for yourselves a better possession and a lasting one.[24]

These saints took joyfully the seizure of their property. They *rejoiced* for the loss because they knew that they had in heaven a better and abiding possession in exact proportion to what was lost. They *knew* it in themselves as a conviction. It was a knowing that was beyond mere doctrinal acknowledgment, and the proof of their knowing was that they took the seizure *joyfully*. Their joy was the statement of their faith in the most acute moment of being stripped. They were a people free from fear and intimidation, and from the security of their possessions. We can know whether eternity is just an abstraction or the deepest reality just by our reaction to being stripped of our earthly goods. Is there a joyful surrendering? There is a difference between bearing something with a brave kind of resignation, as opposed to *counting it all joy*. Joy cannot be feigned. It is a heavenly quality, not some kind of human happiness. Their faith was eschatological; they expected heavenly reward. For them, eternity was the greater and more enduring reality.

> Therefore, do not throw away your confidence, which has a great reward. For you have need of endurance, so that when you have done the will of God, you may receive what was promised.[25]

---

[24] Hebrews 10:32-34
[25] Hebrews 10:35-36

In other words, they did not receive, nor did they expect to receive, the promise until *after* they had done the will of God. That is a strange thing to consider. It means they did not receive in this life the thing for which they gave themselves totally to God. They did not receive the thing for which they were striving in God. They served God tirelessly and totally, without having to have their reward in this life. The world and its rewards did not move them. They were not seduced into accepting honorary biblical doctorates. They had no religious ambition, no need to be acknowledged.

These are the "hidden" saints, who can serve God without being recognized and known by men. We need to be joined with them, in the same quality of faith, instead of looking for the reward that men can bestow presently. True sons of God look to the greater reward. They allow God to ruthlessly deal with them, removing any impulse for a present acknowledgement and reward. Both they, and we, will receive our reward at the same time—in the day of eternity, the day of the Lord's appearing.

"For yet in a very little while, He who is coming will come, and will not delay."[26] Jesus' coming will usher in the day of eternity and reward. It was written two thousand years ago, and the Lord has still not come. Was the writer's use of the phrase "in a little while" an unnecessary exaggeration? It was little, in the same way that Paul saw his afflictions as both momentary and light. It was little because he already anticipated eternity at the door. It was not an issue of chronology, but an issue of God's character, the God who promises: "He who promised *will* come."

---

[26] Hebrews 10:37

Here comes the punch-line: "*Now* the just shall live by faith."[27] Having just written about what comes *after*—the inheritance and the reward—the writer brings the subject into the immediate, present now. In other words, "The just shall live by this eschatological faith in the present now." Will the Lord find *this* kind of faith upon the earth when He returns?

How do we live in the present in a way that is *really* living? How do we live joyfully when anything other than that is not living? This is the paradox of the faith. Having spoken all of those things about *afterwards*, we come to *now*. Now is only now because of what comes after. Now would not be now without the promise and the reward. Now is only now because God is God. Now we can live by faith in the anticipation and confidence of the recompense of the reward that comes after. It gives us the incentive to serve God *now*, eclipsing every other present reward.

> But just as it is written, "Things which eye has not seen and ear has not heard, and which have not entered the heart of man, all that God has prepared for those who love Him."[28]

There is a crown to be won; there is a treasure that is being laid up. The key to overcoming *now* is because of what comes *after*. This alone *is* the faith once and for all given to the saints for which we need earnestly to contend! Faith is a mode of living that takes into its deepest consciousness the eschatological, apocalyptic expectation of the end of the age in its theocratic promise, thereby transforming our quality of

---

[27] Hebrews 10:38 KJV Bible. Emphasis mine.
[28] 1 Corinthians 2:9

life *now*.

We are moving toward a consummation and a hope. What we are now, and how we walk now, are related to what it is that we anticipate for the future. Furthermore, we have a foretaste now of the power and the glory of the age to come because we are given the Holy Spirit as a down payment and foretaste of the power of that age.

One of the terrible things wrong with numbers of contemporary movements is that they have not seen the Holy Spirit in His eschatological context. They have seen the baptism in the Holy Spirit only as a present phenomenon, as something to renew our denominations, bringing a degree of excitement into our otherwise dull and predictable Christian life. They have confused their experience as being the fullness that was to be poured out on all flesh, when it was in reality only a sprinkling and preview of that future event. They have not seen the baptism in the context of God's full cosmic intention for the nations and especially for the nation Israel.

Eternal Reward

This concept of eternal reward is virtually absent from the consideration of most believers today, and may well be a statement of how little we understand the faith. There is an overwhelming testimony of scriptural evidence to suggest that striving to obtain the reward is a remarkably glorious theme central to the faith. The powers of the air profoundly resist this subject, because to lay hold of the issues of eternity will open up a whole dimension of release in the church, thereby allowing it to challenge their false, usurping rule.

Is our present longing for the Lord's coming simply a piece of doctrinal correctness, an inevitable historical necessity, or maybe even something that will be for us an escape from a time of tribulation? Or do we see His coming as the time when we are given the reward appropriate to our service and sacrifice? It makes a great deal of difference, because it will influence how we live *now*. An expectation of a reward is one of the keys to being able to bear persecution and oppression in this life.

> Behold, I am coming quickly, and My reward is with Me, to render to every man according to what he has done.[29]

The rewards, our place in the heavenlies, our level of responsibility with the Lord in the millennial kingdom as those who rule and reign with Him, are proportionate to the quality of our labor and service in *this* life. Some will rule over two cities, some over five and some over ten, showing that there are degrees of reward. Ruling and reigning with Christ is bringing the wisdom of God to bear on a situation that needs it. We exercise this judgment out of the character and stature obtained in *this* life.

> Now he who plants and he who waters are one; but each will receive his own reward according to his own labor.[30]

> Each man's work will become evident; for the day will show it because it is to be

---

[29] Revelation 22:12
[30] 1 Corinthians 3:8

revealed with fire, and the fire itself will test the quality of each man's work. If any man's work which he has built on it remains, he will receive a reward. If any man's work is burned up, he will suffer loss; but he himself will be saved, yet so as through fire.[31]

The issue of eternal distinction is completely a matter of our own desire. It is what we have accomplished or done in this life, by the grace of God that is given, in proportion to our willingness to undertake and perform the works of God. Not every work we do for Him is necessarily *His* work. Merely because a work fulfills a need does not mean that the work will earn for us honor, reward, or distinction. Many of our works will be burned up, being hay, wood and stubble, rather than gold, silver or precious gems. Fire tests the works, and only that which passes through the fire qualifies for eternal reward. The works of God have their inception in Him. They are performed out of the rest of God, out of faithful obedience, out of the willingness to be unknown and unheralded. They are performed by those with pure motives in the power of His life, those who seek His will, purposes and glory.

When we all stand at the judgment seat of Christ, our works will be tested to see whether they can survive the fire of God's evaluation and judgment. Salvation is a gift of God by grace, but what we do with the grace, having obtained it as a gift, determines our eternal place and eternal reward.

---

[31] Ibid., vv.13-15

> Beware of practicing your righteousness before men to be noticed by them; otherwise you have no reward with your Father who is in heaven.[32]

We can lose our reward if our motives are impure. If we want to be seen, recognized and honored by men, we lose the corresponding eternal reward. It is the hope of that reward that will enable us to perform a work, even when people do not acknowledge it, or are not grateful for it. This is a complete reversal of the incentives that most men require; they perform because they want to be seen of men, recognized, and celebrated.

> Blessed are you when people insult you and persecute you, and falsely say all kinds of evil against you because of Me. Rejoice and be glad, for your reward in heaven is great; for in the same way they persecuted the prophets who were before you.[33]

Joy and gladness can be experienced *now*, in the moment of the shame and rejection. Our faith is a living faith; we anticipate the reward in such a way that it is a present factor in our demeanor and conduct. If there is no inner joy[34] in the moment that we suffer disgrace, reproach and rejection for Christ's sake, then we have need of a deeper conversion. If our faith is shallow, superficial or half-hearted, we will move into self-pity and see ourselves as victims of the sins of

---
[32] Matthew 6:1
[33] Matthew 5:11-12
[34] Not to be confused with a joyful emotion, but more to be understood in terms of an inner peace, the product of a life wholly surrendered to the will of God.

another.

The anticipation of a reward that does not fade away, does not rust, and which cannot be stolen, is designed by God to be one of the most powerful compelling motives for our present service. It was an enormous factor in Moses' own overcoming life and separation from Egypt, symbolic of the world:

> By faith Moses, when he had grown up, refused to be called the son of Pharaoh's daughter, choosing rather to endure ill-treatment with the people of God than to enjoy the passing pleasures of sin, considering the reproach of Christ greater riches than the treasures of Egypt; for he was looking to the reward.[35]

THE TWO RESURRECTIONS

> Then I saw thrones, and they sat on them, and judgment was given to them. And I saw the souls of those who had been beheaded because of their testimony of Jesus and because of the word of God, and those who had not worshiped the beast or the image, and had not received the mark on their forehead and on their hand; and they came to life and reigned with Christ for a thousand years. The rest of the dead did not come to life until the thousand years were completed. This is the first

---

[35] Hebrews 11:24-26

resurrection.[36]

Believers do not all rise at the same time. Some will rise with the first resurrection, a "first fruits" entity. These will rule and reign with Him in His millennial kingdom. Others will sleep through the millennium, and only rise with the general resurrection of the dead.

Some of us will not be equipped to rule and reign with Christ, because we have ignored, or forsaken, or have had no stomach for the kind of responsibility that would fit us for such a role. If we have been content to sit passively in fellowships our entire Christian life because we were assured that we were "going to heaven," we may well be profoundly disappointed to find we are not in that glorious first resurrection.

> Blessed and holy is the one who has a part in the first resurrection; over these the second death has no power, but they will be priests of God and of Christ and will reign with Him for a thousand years.[37]

The wording in these verses could not be clearer. The word "first" implies that there is another resurrection to follow, and those who did not rise in the first resurrection are "the rest of the dead," whose rising is at a later time.

The character of those who strove to obtain the first resurrection are mentioned as being blessed, holy and priestly. They came to that quality *before* their resurrection. It is clear that not every believer is blessed, holy and priestly. This is the resurrection that

---
[36] Revelation 20:4-5
[37] Revelation 20:6

Paul strove to obtain, and which we also need to strive for. We are not going to be blessed, holy and priestly if we are presently giving ourselves to the gratification of the flesh. It is going to take a disciplined, submitted life, one that is submitted both to God and to other brethren. It is a life that will joyfully receive correction rather than balking and reacting in resentment when that correction comes. It is a life submitted to the cross in truth.

It is not only the liars and gross sinners that are kept out of the kingdom, but also the cowardly. What we desire in this life will either condemn us or exalt us to a place of rule in the life to come. There is a finality about the day of judgment. From my own reading of the scriptures, it seems that every single aspect of reward is decided in *this* life.

Those who rise in the first resurrection are they whom Jesus referred to when He said to Nathaniel:

> Truly, truly, I say to you, you will see the heavens opened and the angels of God ascending and descending on the Son of Man.[38]

In their administration of the kingdom, they will have glorified bodies, able to move through walls, just as Jesus did in His glorified body. It is their privilege and their reward to be co-administrators with the Lord. This is not government as we traditionally know it; it is heavenly and divine rule, the goodness and wisdom of God teaching men how to live in righteousness, mediated in the meekness of the Lamb. There is no higher honor than to rule and reign with Christ in His

---

[38] John 1:51b

theocratic kingdom. Ruling was Jesus' reward, for which a throne was prepared for Him. God not only raised Him from the dead, but raised Him up on high, to a place of rule, where all authority has been given to Him both in heaven and in earth.

> Then I saw a great white throne and Him who sat upon it, from whose presence earth and heaven fled away, and no place was found for them. And I saw the dead, the great and the small, standing before the throne, and books were opened; and another book was opened, which is the book of life; and the dead were judged from the things which were written in the books, according to their deeds. And the sea gave up the dead which were in it, and death and Hades gave up the dead which were in them; and they were judged, every one of them according to their deeds. Then death and Hades were thrown into the lake of fire. This is the second death, the lake of fire. And if anyone's name was not found written in the book of life, he was thrown into the lake of fire.[39]

From a simple and literal reading of that text, those who were not qualified to rise with the blessed, holy and priestly saints had to wait a thousand years. They missed the initiation of God's kingdom and any participation in it. We have to deduce that there must have been a number of those who *were* saved, but who lived lives without any significant distinction that would have earned them the reward of a first

---

[39] Revelation 20:11-15

resurrection. They were therefore to be judged with all the other dead who do not rise with the first resurrection—otherwise there would be no need to consult the Lamb's book of life. Those who rise in the first resurrection reveal the approval and acceptance of being found *in* Christ. Their walk, conduct, character and works qualify them for the resurrection. They are "found worthy."

Those whose names are found in the Lamb's book of life at the second resurrection are going to be saved from being thrown into the lake of fire with all the rest of the dead, but I would not want to wait to see if my name was written in that book. There is a possibility that it might have been written, but has since been blotted out. Paul was intensely desirous of that first resurrection. Unless we have his same determination, we will not be found worthy of that same privilege.

> And the nations were enraged, and Your wrath came, and the time came for the dead to be judged, and the time to reward Your bond-servants the prophets and the saints and those who fear Your name, the small and the great, and to destroy those who destroy the earth.[40]

Here is the judgment of God, destroying those who destroy, but giving reward both *small* and *great*. There is reward at every level, and at every grade, proportionate to our works. To be without reward will be an eternal shame.

---

[40] Revelation 11:18

The Judgment Seat of Christ

> For the Son of Man is going to come in the glory of His Father with His angels, and will then repay every man according to his deeds.[41]

> And I will kill her children with pestilence, and all the churches will know that I am He who searches the minds and hearts; and I will give to each one of you according to your deeds.[42]

It is out of the mouth of the Lord Himself, showing again that our reward is an individual matter.

> For we must all appear before the judgment seat of Christ, so that each one may be recompensed for his deeds in the body, according to what he has done, whether good or bad.[43]

Here we see one of the principal incentives to walk in a particular way in this life with regard to our body. What do we give our minds to? What kind of thoughts do we allow, thinking we have the luxury to contemplate them, even though no one else hears them or sees them? It is still done in our body.

> But you, why do you judge your brother? Or you again, why do you regard your brother with contempt? For we will all stand before the judgment seat of God.[44]

---

[41] Matthew 16:27
[42] Revelation 2:23
[43] 2 Corinthians 5:10
[44] Romans 14:10

If we know that we are going to stand before God and give account, then we should not ourselves be disposed to be judgmental. That is the meaning of the scripture that says, "Do not judge." Those who judge themselves need not be judged of God. We need to be ruthless with ourselves and examine our hearts, and ask the Lord for illumination and light that we may see the truth of our condition, be broken for it, and repent for it *now*.

> He who overcomes will thus be clothed in white garments; and I will not erase his name from the book of life, and I will confess his name before My Father and before His angels.[45]

In other words, names will be erased from the Lamb's book of life. This is a jolt to the "eternal security" doctrine that many in the church have adopted for themselves. But it helps to explain the slack attitude that is to be found in the lives of many today, unwilling for the sacrifice required for overcoming or obtaining a priestly stature in God, and thinking that somehow we will have the same heaven, the same resurrection and the same reward as everyone else. The scriptures show that God gives rewards proportionate to the quality of character and service performed and obtained in *this* life. We may well find that when we stand before Him, who is Truth, that there might be another eternal verdict different from what we had naïvely expected, and in that moment, and from thenceforth, it is eternally fixed.

---

[45] Revelation 3:5

The Millennial Kingdom

Eternal reward is set in the context of a literal coming kingdom on the earth. The Lord is going to establish a kingdom of righteousness for the first time since creation. The law of the Lord and His word shall go out from Jerusalem to the nations, and the nations shall learn righteousness.[46] This will take men and women who are already skilled in the issues of righteousness, and who can bring benevolent influence to a situation. For this task, they will have glorified bodies, ascending and descending upon the Son of Man, being directed where needed, and aiding Israel's influence and witness as the evangelistic nation.

Restored Israel is not the administrator of the coming kingdom. The risen, glorified church administers the kingdom. It is the church, the saints, the called-out ones from every generation, who rule and reign with Christ. Israel will be the *subjects* of the kingdom in the same way that they were under King David. This time they will be subjects under the Greater David, the Lord Himself, who will be their Prince and Ruler forever. They will make known the gospel of the kingdom in the same sense that the church today promulgates the gospel, but the actual administration and establishment of the rule of God in the earth is reserved as a privilege for the overcoming saints. They have been given the right to be co-rulers by virtue of their sacrifice, character and conduct while they were on the earth.

---

[46] See Isaiah 2:2-4. See also author's book: *The Mystery of Israel and the Church*

The powers of the air strive to keep the church in its present lackluster, uninspired and matter-of-fact condition, because if it remains like that, it is not likely to rise in the first resurrection; it will not respond to the trumpet of God and to the voice of the Lord, for it did not respond to His voice in this life. The powers do not want to see the kingdom come because the establishment of that kingdom means the end of their false, usurping rule.

This expectation of a "kingdom come," of a literal, political rule of God over His creation, is the promise for which the great saints of old sacrificed, suffered and died. They were heirs to the promise of a kingdom. Eternal reward is millennial reward; it is participation in the millennial kingdom. If we cannot conceive of that kingdom, and have no anticipation for it, and think of it only as an abstraction, and do not have a faith to believe for it, then the talk of reward is altogether vain. That ancient cry of the church, "Come, Lord Jesus" was in the anticipation of a coming King to establish His kingdom. It should also be *our* hope; it is the blessed hope of the church, and given as an incentive to be found blameless and worthy in the day of His coming.

Are we anticipating the Lord's pronouncement over us as being, "well done, good and faithful servant"? In whatever small thing we are laboring in, are our motives pure? Are we being good stewards, multiplying the little we were given? Are our works performed in the fulfillment of His will? Only *that* is a true work. When we do something out of our own human energy, even though we do it for the Lord, it is totally unacceptable to Him. Everything must be *of*

Him, *through* Him in order that it might be glory *unto* Him forever. The whole key is being dead and hidden with Christ in God. It is a humiliation to be dead, and if we are not willing for that suffering, we cannot expect that our works will endure.

The Invisible Cloud of Witnesses

> Therefore, since we have so great a cloud of witnesses surrounding us, let us also lay aside every encumbrance and the sin which so easily entangles us, and let us run with endurance the race that is set before us.[47]

It is a great assurance and comfort to know that the saints who have preceded us, in this very same precious faith, are waiting for us to come to the finish line. They have not yet received their reward, because they are not yet made perfect without us. They are present in an invisible cloud, exerting from that place a positive influence to encourage us on to the conclusion of the race that is set before us. They are a vital ingredient of a very particular kind to facilitate the glorious conclusion of the age *through* us. We are in a continuum with all of the saints who have preceded us, those who were of *this* faith. Do we see ourselves, now and presently, in that context? We are in something together that links the past with the eternal future. We are moving toward something to which they have already sacrificed and given themselves, but which will not be obtained independently of us.

---

[47] Hebrews 12:1

Entering His Rest

In the book of Hebrews, Paul gives an illustration or type from the Old Testament of those who failed to enter into the land of promise. Those who went out of Egypt and into the wilderness came under the blood of the lamb, and passed through the waters of baptism *into* Moses. However, that whole generation, except for Joshua and Caleb, died in the wilderness without entering the land of promise. They failed to enter into the rest that God had prepared. It is a very sober warning, for it is apparent that we can come under the blood of the Lamb, pass through the waters of baptism, and yet not enter into the land of promise. In a very real sense, the land of promise is a prefiguring of the kingdom of God, for that is where the literal kingdom, its crown and throne are to be established. The Israelites under Moses were forbidden to enter the land because of their lack of faith; they did not have the anticipation or desire.

> All the sons of Israel grumbled against Moses and Aaron; and the whole congregation said to them, "Would that we had died in the land of Egypt! Or would that we had died in this wilderness! Why is the LORD bringing us into this land, to fall by the sword? Our wives and our little ones will become plunder; would it not be better for us to return to Egypt?"[48]

---

[48] Numbers 14:2-3

They actually despised the land of promise in the same way that we can despise the eternal reward. They did not take it to heart; they did not *long* for the reward or count it of any consequence. They did not want to contemplate the difficulty of what coming into that land would require. Those who enter the land are willing to share in the humiliations and sufferings of Christ. It is not a picnic to go through the wilderness and into the land of promise, fighting and overcoming all of the Canaanite cities. It is a struggle and a suffering. We will not be willing to make that journey unless we believe the land is an exceedingly great reward. The Israelites did not think the land was sufficient compensation for the sacrifice they knew they would be required to make. The cowardly shall not enter the kingdom.

> But My servant Caleb, because he has had a different spirit and has followed Me fully, I will bring into the land which he entered, and his descendants shall take possession of it.[49]

This is more than the physical descendants of Caleb, and would include those who are of like mind, heart and spirit with him. Those who are casual, shallow and complacent are not of the seed of Caleb. They will not share in the reward. Caleb had a fervent spirit that was wholehearted toward God. He wanted the *entire* reward. Indeed, if we are not wholehearted, which is what the name "Caleb" means, we will not be fitted to rule and reign with Christ in His kingdom.

Do not harden your hearts as when they

---

[49] Numbers 14:24

> provoked Me, as in the day of trial in the wilderness, where your fathers tried Me by testing Me, and saw My works for forty years.[50]

Israel provoked the Lord because they despised the excellent land and were not willing for the sacrifice to enter it.

> Therefore I was angry with this generation, and said, "They always go astray in their heart, and they did not know My ways"; as I swore in My wrath, 'They shall not enter My rest.'" Take care, brethren, that there not be in any one of you an evil, unbelieving heart that falls away from the living God.[51]

In other words, take care that you also are not half-hearted, that you also are unwilling to obtain the full measure.

> For we have become partakers of Christ, if we hold fast the beginning of our assurance firm until the end.[52]

That is to say, we have become partakers of His kingdom and reign, but only if we hold fast, and not give up.

> And to whom did He swear that they would not enter His rest, but to those who were disobedient? So we see that they were not able to enter because of unbelief.[53]

---

[50] Hebrews 3:8-9
[51] Hebrews 3:10-12
[52] Ibid., v.14
[53] Ibid., vv.18-19

They did not have a *heart* for that which God was making available. They did not embrace the faith as it was presented to them.

> Therefore, let us fear if, while a promise remains of entering His rest, any one of you may seem to have come short of it.[54]

You come short of what might have been your eternal joy as a reward.

> For indeed we have had good news preached to us, just as they also; but the word they heard did not profit them, because it was not united by faith in those who heard.[55]

They heard the report of the spies, but they did not hear it with faith. We can hear something, and be just as guilty, if it is not united with faith. The word is without profit unless something comes out from us to receive and take it to heart.

Faith is not faith in the sense of a collection of doctrines. Faith is a disposition of spirit that wants to activate and realize the thing that has been spoken. The Israelites of that time had no intention or desire to see the promise of God fulfilled. God therefore condemns them, because it was something in which *they* had failed, not something in which *God* had failed. He gave them the land of promise. The good report was given. The word was preached, but they failed and refused to receive the word so as to do it. Therefore, His anger was kindled against them:

> For we who have believed enter that rest,

---

[54] Hebrews 4:1
[55] Hebrews 4:2

just as He has said, "As I swore in My wrath, they shall not enter My rest," although His works were finished from the foundation of the world.[56]

Being brought out of the bondage of Egypt does not automatically give you entry into the promised land. It is exactly the same with God's people today. There are those who have no millennial or eternal expectation. They make up those who are rooted in the present. They can believe for the "manna" that comes down *now*, but cannot believe for the thing that is future, distant or eternal. The failure to believe was the disqualification for entering the land, and it is exactly the same for any of us. To have no millennial or eternal expectation is to be excluded from its fulfillment and from any participation in the promised kingdom.

In their grumbling, the Israelites showed something that revealed where they in fact *were*, and where we in fact *are*, for exactly the same reason:

> All the sons of Israel grumbled against Moses and Aaron; and the whole congregation said to them, "Would that we had died in the land of Egypt! Or would that we had died in this wilderness! Why is the LORD bringing us into this land, to fall by the sword? Our wives and our little ones will become plunder; would it not be better for us to return to Egypt?"[57]

Those who had no heart to enter were occupied

---

[56] Ibid., v.3
[57] Numbers 14:2-3

only with their own well-being and self-interest. Those who were willing for the sacrifice of going through the wilderness to enter the promised land were occupied with the glory of God. The coming kingdom is the issue of God's glory, and if we are preoccupied with our own security, comfort and gratification, we will prefer Egypt, though we might not say it in so many words. Caleb and Joshua had a decidedly different motive. For them, the coming into the promised land was not for the benefits that would accrue to them; it was for the glory that would accrue to God.

> Or do you not know that the unrighteous will not inherit the kingdom of God? Do not be deceived; neither fornicators, nor idolaters, nor adulterers, nor effeminate, nor homosexuals, nor thieves, nor the covetous, nor drunkards, nor revilers, nor swindlers, will inherit the kingdom of God.[58]

The Corinthian church was already marked by moral failures. Paul made it clear to them that they would not inherit the kingdom of God if they continued to be characterized by unrighteousness.

EXCOMMUNICATION

Excommunication from fellowship has very little meaning for most of us today. In apostolic times, to be expelled and excommunicated from fellowship was to be cut off from both God and the life of God. It was such a feared penalty because it was a preview of what

---

[58] 1 Corinthians 6:9-10

expulsion from the kingdom would *eternally* mean. The one excommunicated would come into a very real experience of "outer darkness." He would feel what it would be like to be cut off from an eternal fellowship with the saints of God and from God Himself. Excommunication, when rightly practiced, is a mercy from God. We are given to consider something *in this life* of what our eternal penalty will be if we remain unrepentant. If our sin is worthy of excommunication, we are also candidates for expulsion from the kingdom of God.

In making known the issues of eternity *in this present life*, the church has a great responsibility to convey the full council of God. It needs to recognize a repentance that will enable men's sins to be forgiven. By the same token, it needs to withhold the forgiveness of the sins of the unrepentant. If they are withheld here on earth, they are also withheld in heaven. If someone is excommunicated *here*, they are excommunicated *there*. The church is the agent God intended to determine where men would occupy themselves in eternity. If God excluded an entire Israel from entering for their unbelief, how will He flinch from excluding believers, for the same reason, to their eternal lament?

In the moment of eternity, in the day of the Lord, we will find that what we might have dismissed and despised is actually true. We will then have to eternally forfeit something that cannot be remedied. We are fixed permanently in the outer darkness, not only without reward, but also without fellowship of a kind that would have made eternity a joy.

The Apocalyptic View and "Blessed Hope" of the Church

The distinctive of true church is that it has an apocalyptic view, a dynamic of expectancy of the imminent coming of the Lord as Judge and King. The issue is not *when* the Lord returns, but the *faithfulness* of the God who promised His return. The apocalyptic mindset is the belief that Satan's evil influence and rule will be ended by the direct intervention of God. The scriptures tell us that the whole world lies in the power of Satan. The only end for such a false rule is by being cast out. Indeed, the Lord's coming *will* end Satan's usurping rule over God's creation

The most offensive message to communicate to mankind is to tell them that this world is under judgment, that its end is near, that there is a coming fire and that they had better know *now* the soon-coming King. In the day of His coming, it will be too late to make His acquaintance because He is coming as Judge rather than Savior. It is an unwelcome message because everything that men do in the world suggests perpetuity rather than an end.

Furthermore, if we preach the gospel of the kingdom in power and anointing, we will have men rush upon us with bared teeth. Any gospel that is not in the apocalyptic context of a soon-coming kingdom with a Judge is not the gospel of God. A vital content and dynamic has been lost which no longer makes it the gospel of the kingdom. Inherent in the apocalyptic gospel is a particular urgency, an expectation and a hope.

> For the grace of God has appeared, bringing salvation to all men, instructing us to deny ungodliness and worldly desires and to live sensibly, righteously and godly in the present age, looking for the blessed hope and the appearing of the glory of our great God and Savior, Christ Jesus, who gave Himself for us to redeem us from every lawless deed, and to purify for Himself a people for His own possession, zealous for good deeds. These things speak and exhort and reprove with all authority. Let no one disregard you.[59]

This is another one of those great apostolic summations of the faith. We anticipate the Lord's appearing and the coming of another kingdom, yet, while we are waiting, we are zealous for good works. There is a present application. The apocalyptic view brings requirements in this present life. We are living in a transitory time, loaded with great purposes, but it is to be lived in the expectation of the great conclusion to the age. In the increasing darkness around us, the witness of the church is to be a light set on a hill, a visible demonstration of the kingdom that is to come. The church is God's final mercy to save souls from eternal darkness. If that witness is refused, they are refusing a last grace God offers to a dying world. Therefore, the church has all the more obligation to live blamelessly and without reproach in this present age.

---

[59] Titus 2:11-15

Denying worldly lusts does not mean avoiding sexual orgies. A lust could be anything as innocuous as a preoccupation with a merchandising flyer for the local supermarket. How will it affect us if we no longer have access to it? Do we *have* to have it? If denial is too painful for your flesh to consider, it is already a lust. There is a power in merchandise that is seductive. It seeks to pull us into its vortex and captivate our souls. The variety and stimulation of merchandise will rob us of the eternal perspective. We see others with it, we see how they approve it, or use it, or wear it. Eventually, we must have it, and we thereby succumb to worldly lust.

To live soberly is to live carefully, avoiding those things that have an injurious affect upon our spirit. The way in which food is exhibited in a supermarket is calculated to influence the customer toward worldly lusts. Shelves are arranged to induce us to take items that we would have never ordinarily purchased. Even the high volume of merchandise on the shelves does something to our carnal desire and appetite. God has given us the "blessed hope" to sustain us when the pressures of merchandise come upon us. It is a hope of a particular kind that has sustained the saints of every generation.

The powers of the air cannot abide those who anticipate a kingdom other than their own. Wherever there is an anticipation of an end and a new future, an eternal reign different from this world, we will experience some form of opposition from those same powers. Many will find themselves stripped of their earthly goods; but if we are stripped, we can praise God, rejoicing that it could not have happened without the Lord's permission, knowing that in heaven there is a yet greater and enduring substance and reward. If we cannot take the stripping of our goods with joy, we are, to that degree, distanced from the blessed hope. In other words, those goods were for us the result of a worldly lust.

> Now may the God of hope fill you with all joy and peace in believing, so that you will abound in hope by the power of the Holy Spirit.[60]

It begins with the word *now*. Biblical hope has to do with an expectancy for the future, but if hope does not have a consequence that is immediate and present, it is not hope. The uniqueness of the faith is that the things which are future have an immediate and practical consequence *now*. The very nature of the faith is to abound. Anything less than abounding is abnormal and substandard. The joy of the Lord comes from heaven. It is *with* God, and it is inextricably joined with abounding in hope.

Hope is the anticipation of something future. Hope is the belief that one day we are going to appropriate that which is yet invisible and distant. We cannot be holy or perfect without hope. Hope is the ingredient by which we believe we are going to be made perfect *in* Him. True hope is active, palpitating, vital and alive. No matter what the circumstance, no matter what the present discouragement, hope is the element by which we remain steadfast and immovable.

---

[60] Romans 15:13

MOCKERS AND SCOFFERS IN THE LAST DAYS

> Know this first of all, that in the last days mockers will come with their mocking, following after their own lusts, and saying, "Where is the promise of His coming? For ever since the fathers fell asleep, all continues just as it was from the beginning of creation."[61]

Mocking, or scoffing, is an attitude of contempt, disdain and cynicism. Much more than we know, scoffing is a consequence of our lusts, and our theology will be affected accordingly.

Though we subscribe to the doctrine of the Lord's coming, it is not a vibrant hope for many of us, especially if we think this world is not such a bad place after all. We have a nice home, security and comfort. If there are any problems, we have a certain optimism that they will improve. We are not looking for another reality, and our tendency is to embrace the things that reinforce or comfort us in the mode of life that we have chosen. Our view of the faith is very much determined by how we choose to live our life here on earth.

The scoffers that Peter is talking about are not the scoffers in the world, but in the church. If we want to keep our theology and doctrines pure, then we need to examine our lifestyles. What is there in them that would compromise us? What is there that we want to see perpetuated that would be threatened by an end? If we want our lifestyles to continue, we are not going to embrace with enthusiasm an apocalyptic view that says

---

[61] 2 Peter 3:3-4

there is an end. We will find a way either to deny the Lord's literal coming to the earth, or we will give only a cerebral, outward and ceremonial acknowledgment of it. Even though we are able to have a standard of living that we can afford, does our expectancy of the things to come justify that lifestyle? Can we voluntarily simplify our lifestyle in keeping with the view of a soon-coming end?

A lifestyle of excess and self-indulgence is not compatible with the apocalyptic view. Discipline is not forced upon us, but something which we voluntarily take upon ourselves. Why should we give ourselves to the values established by the gods of this world, seeing that they are soon to be unseated and defeated in the Lord's own coming? The apocalyptic view calls us to a seriousness about how we presently live. It is a call to blamelessness, all the more in a world that is becoming more sinful and corrupt.

Daniel refused to eat at the king's table. That table would have been a sumptuous, elaborate and lavish extravagance, as well as a sensual delight. If Daniel had eaten at that table, as the false prophets ate from the table of Jezebel, he would not have been the instrument of God to receive a revelation of the mysteries of God. The book of Daniel begins, significantly, with his refusal to eat from that table. If we are going to take a posture that is in opposition to a world that is under judgment, everything about our lifestyle needs to be under careful scrutiny. While everyone else is striving to obtain the things that boost their lifestyle, can we impose upon ourselves a voluntary discipline, and simplify our lifestyle by resisting what is available, even the things we consider legitimate?

There is an actual blessedness in looking for the blessed hope of the appearing of the Lord. How many of us today can say that we have a blessed hope that sustains us, and enables us to bear whatever form of suffering it would please the Lord to mete out to us? How many of us turned the blessed hope into a "rapture" theory as an escape from the things that are soon to come upon the earth? That is not the biblical hope at all.

Apocalyptic Scenario

Why is it that two thousand years later the hope of the Lord's coming has not yet materialized? Was the early church believing a fiction, an exaggerated view? Who wants to contemplate an end where the earth melts with a fervent heat and the stars fall out of their place? A cataclysmic shaking of creation itself is not something that our flesh wants to consider, but it is a necessary ingredient in the whole apocalyptic picture.

There will be a final devastation and shaking, and the only thing that will make one capable of bearing such an event is the joy from knowing what follows, because out of it comes a new heaven and a new earth wherein righteousness dwells. A new heaven and a new earth are only made necessary because the old heaven[62] and the old earth are caught up in the final devastation of God's judgment whereby they are purified. God's creation is not going to be obliterated and replaced. Rather, the righteousness of God is

---

[62] i.e., the heavenlies

going to transfigure both the earth and the heavens, and out of that purification, there will be one new and enduring entity.

For the early believers, an expectation of an imminent end was a compelling reason for those who had land and houses to sell them, and lay the proceeds at the feet of the apostles, who would then distribute it to those in need. What is the point in hanging on to your property if the end is near and at hand? Having this mindset gives you a certain release, and enables you to come into a largesse of spirit instead of clutching something to keep for the future. If the future is now, and the age is at an end, and the Lord is coming, it is better to give up our possessions, and employ them for the purposes of God in the church's final activity than to embarrassingly be sitting on it when the Lord comes, when it will have no value at all.

Those early believers were not deceived to believe in an imminent end. Why would God allow them to have a mentality like that, since what they expected did not materialize? Was God allowing His people to expect something that *could not* come about that quickly? Is God Himself an agent of deception? Definitely not, but in that dynamic of expectation, a certain living, a certain faith and laying up of treasure in heaven takes place. Apocalyptic expectancy has always been God's normative intention for the church in *every* generation.

The world is becoming increasingly inhospitable for the true people of God. If it were not for the hope of the faith, we ourselves would despair. We need, therefore, to have in our consciousness the perspective that was central to the church's life from the beginning, and which needs again to be restored.

> Since all these things are to be destroyed in this way, what sort of people ought you to be in holy conduct and godliness, looking for and hastening the coming of the day of God, because of which the heavens will be destroyed by burning, and the elements will melt with intense heat![63]

We ought to *long* for the day of His appearing. We who seek Him with that longing are contributing to the hastening of the day of His appearing. If that is so, we can actually hasten the Lord's appearing by our character and lively anticipation. The prospect of a glorious reward accentuates that desire for the Lord's coming. The hope is blessed, because it gives the enablement to bear what one must. It is a confident expectation with the prospect of a glorious reward. You cannot explain Christian martyrdom outside of the hope for eternal reward. The fact that believers of the past went to their deaths joyously was one of the most profound testimonies of the truth of their faith. Their persecutors saw people who were not at all alarmed by the prospect of death, and who bore it with great patience, and even with joy, because they saw the reward, by the Spirit, that was being prepared for them.

The Lord is at the door. The world is coming to its historic end. God is going to break into time to conclude history, and to begin the reign of the Lamb. If that for us is not real and urgent, we will covet what we have; we will hang on to our investments and retirement plans. If we do not live as if we believe the

---

[63] 2 Peter 3:11-12

Lord is coming, our witness both to the Jew and to the Gentile is thereby distorted. We miss a central, foundational prop that ought to be part of our whole perception of life. Let us not reduce the faith to just a compendium of dry-as-dust doctrines to which we mentally subscribe. God would have the church of every generation to *live* in the expectancy of an end. Nothing has changed, and that is what we need to see.

CHAPTER 3

Apostolic Realities: The Principalities and Powers of the Air

An understanding of the principalities and the powers of the air is foundational to all true seeing. There is a realm of invisible, angelic beings brooding over this earth, profoundly influencing the conduct of individuals and nations. They are the rulers of this present world. It is extraordinary how naïve, ignorant, or indifferent the church is toward these powers, *despite* the fact that this theme is absolutely foundational to the whole calling of the church!

> For our struggle is not against flesh and blood, but against the rulers, against the powers, against the world forces of this darkness, against the spiritual forces of

wickedness in the heavenly places.[1]

God's people are called to be engaged in a struggle that has been going on for thousands of years. It is a cosmic conflict between the kingdom of darkness and the kingdom of God. If we think that the subject of demons is only the issue of personal deliverance, we have missed the *greater* importance. The focus on deliverance has fixed the understanding of believers at *that* level, and thereby robbed them of the greater and truer understanding of the conflict, namely, the contention for the actual dominion or possession of creation and the nations. Perhaps the strategy of the powers is to have us occupied at the level of personal deliverance rather than combat in the cosmic sense. There is a final defeat that needs to be inflicted upon them by virtue of the church being the church in the true apostolic sense.

If our church life is essentially a place where people come to attend services as an isolated conglomeration of individuals, then it is not equipped for this struggle. Unless there is corporate unity: one heart, one mind and one spirit, we cannot participate in this struggle. This is why the powers will do anything to divide fellowships of believers. They want to keep the church from becoming the corporate expression of the life of God that can wrestle against them.

THE FALL

This cosmic struggle has gone on since the beginning of time. The powers were created by God

---

[1] Ephesians 6:12

for His own purposes. They rebelled against their Creator, and one third of them followed their prince[2] and have become a fallen angelic order. These fallen angels still maintain their governmental places in the heavenlies. God had created this governmental realm to sustain creation, but the powers function today in opposition to what was divinely and originally assigned them. They behave as though *they* were the ultimate ground and reason for being.

The powers are characteristically cynical and unbelieving, profoundly egotistical and vain. Though God says they will meet defeat, they act with a presumption and arrogance contrary to what God says concerning their fate and destiny.

> But you [Satan] said in your heart, "I will ascend to heaven; I will raise my throne above the stars of God, and I will sit on the mount of assembly in the recesses of the north. I will ascend above the heights of the clouds; I will make myself like the Most High."[3]

To which God answers, "Nevertheless you will be thrust down to Sheol, to the recesses of the pit."[4] This angelic host has the same proud character of Satan himself, and will suffer the same eternal fate in the lake of fire.

Though they were intended as a benevolent influence, they have taken to themselves their own purposes. Satan seeks to be deified, to be "as God," and to turn the loyalties and attention of men to

---

[2] Known as Satan or the Devil
[3] Isaiah 14:13-14
[4] Ibid., v.15

himself. He has sought to establish his own values contrary to God's, and thus turn men *away* from God. In other words, the powers have used their governmental place for themselves, and have become the gods of this world.

You say, "Just how influential are these powers?" They were sufficiently influential to crucify the Messiah of Israel:

> Yet we do speak wisdom among those who are mature; a wisdom, however, not of this age nor of the rulers of this age, who are passing away; but we speak God's wisdom in a mystery, the hidden wisdom which God predestined before the ages to our glory; the wisdom which none of the rulers of this age has understood; for if they had understood it they would not have crucified the LORD of glory.[5]

The powers operate through earthly authorities. They expressed their rule and wisdom *through* Pontius Pilate and *through* the Jewish Sanhedrin. In other words, they expressed themselves through the very best of civil and religious government. Roman law and Jewish religion conspired together to crucify the Son of God. They acted out of the wisdom of the powers, a wisdom that employs force, intimidation and threat of death. The crucifixion of Jesus was a hidden wisdom in the intention of God. In being slain from the foundations of the world, God foresaw and ordained that His Son would come and die, but it was a hidden wisdom that the powers could not understand.

---

[5] 1 Corinthians 2:6-8

The Cosmic Setting

Not many of us think in cosmic terms. We have some interest in our own nation and its geographical location, but cosmic is beyond all of these categories, yet it includes them all. The apostolic view is the cosmic view, which sees the all-encompassing setting of the redemptive work of God in creation as described in Paul's letter to the Ephesians:

> To me, the very least of all saints, this grace was given, to preach to the Gentiles the unfathomable riches of Christ, and to bring to light what is the administration of the mystery which for ages has been hidden in God who created all things; so that the manifold wisdom of God might now be made known through the church to the rulers and the authorities in the heavenly places. This was in accordance with the eternal purpose which He carried out in Christ Jesus our Lord, in whom we have boldness and confident access through faith in Him.[6]

God has an eternal purpose that ought to revolutionize our entire perspective about the faith. He has a purpose that is solely and exclusively for the satisfaction of His own heart. Moreover, this purpose is so important to God that He created all things in order that this purpose might be carried out, and that an

---

[6] Ephesians 3:8-12

entity we call the church would be the agent to administer and fulfill this purpose.

It is a grotesque distortion to imagine that the church has been established by God to pander to the needs of mankind by establishing programs and services they consider important for themselves. Until the church takes to itself the eternal purpose of God, and looks to the fulfilling of it, it never will have a true foundation in God. Once it has embraced the purpose of God, it will be freed from the necessity to have programs, or to do anything else to justify its existence by meeting the needs that are everywhere about it.

God created all things in order that through the church the manifold wisdom of God might be made known to the powers. This is the *eternal* purpose of God for the church. Those who ignore the eternal purpose of God, who do not give themselves to that purpose as their first and foremost purpose for being, are not the church in the truest sense of that word. The church that is indifferent to the eternal purpose of God, even though it is impressive in every other way, is not the church in any apostolic and prophetic sense, which is to say, not in any authentic sense.

In order to be the church that is the church in truth, we must embrace the eternal purpose of God, even though we might not see any immediate or practical benefit for doing so. In fact, we will find that God's purpose does not in any way serve *our* purposes. His purpose is a mystery that has to do with a demonstration to be made to the powers of the air. The church that is willing to make *this* demonstration is thereby making known the manifold wisdom of God. This *is* in itself the wisdom of God.

In this context, the biblical meaning of wisdom is the moral values of God. The wisdom, or mentality, of this world is predicated upon self-interest and practicality. It says, "What is the benefit for me if I do this? What is in it for *me*? How is my self-interest secure?" But the wisdom of God is altogether sacrificial. It does not rest on the benefit that one receives for oneself, but on the benefit that *God* receives for Himself. Without that all-embracing dynamic, we will be doomed to a spiritual egotism, and will view things in a way that only affects *us* and *our* interests.

Self-interest, even in things we would call spiritual, is a power that needs to be broken. We will know when that power no longer has a grip on us to the degree we joyfully embrace a purpose greater than and other than ourselves, namely, the eternal purpose of God. The wisdom of the world will say, "That is nonsense. You cannot do that. It is irrational and contradictory to nature itself. Self-interest and survival are the very fundamental principles of life. God helps those who help themselves. Have your happiness, *now*, in this life; that is what life is all about."

If you willingly embrace a purpose that has nothing to do with your own benefit, making *that* your foremost reason for being, you are demonstrating the wisdom of God. This wisdom was perfectly demonstrated at the cross by the Son of Man Himself! In behalf of another, He gave up any interest in His own life and satisfaction. In other words, the ability to lay down one's life, to not consider that life dear, *is* the wisdom of God. It is a wisdom predicated on weakness and foolishness. One wisdom lives for itself, its own preservation and its own advantage. God's wisdom lives for the will of another; it is a selfless wisdom. Jesus never initiated anything out of Himself for His own purposes, but lived entirely for the gratification of His Father.

The powers influence mankind to respond in ways that enhance their own self-interest. This can be just as prevalent in the ministerial world, where many attend Bible School in order to become credentialized, thereby establishing their future ministry. The ministry is seen as a career in which their security is established. As long as we are affected or ruled by self-interest, we have nothing with which to defeat the powers.

"Come down and we will believe you," said the crowd to Jesus. If He had come down, thereby seeking His self-interest and the preservation of His life, He would have contradicted the wisdom of God. Remaining impaled on the cross unto death was a demonstration of the wisdom of God that defeated the powers.

THE CLASH OF TWO WISDOMS

The two wisdoms will always be in collision. The wisdom of God is what God is in Himself, and therefore it is what the church must demonstrate in itself; namely, who and what God is in His essential being. This is what Jesus did in His earthly walk. Everything He did was for the purpose of the Father, without regard for Himself, even though it resulted in His own suffering and death. The church is called to a corporate demonstration of the same wisdom, requiring an earnest, daily relationship and a growing up together. This is something more than the casual conglomeration of believers meeting for a Sunday service.

To think we can "shout down" the powers in Jesus' name when we are still bound in self-interest is a contradiction in terms. The powers of the air are only too glad when we remain verbal in expressing biblical concepts. However, when they see the authenticity of the crucified life and character in believers, which is to say, the very resurrection life of God Himself in His own nature, then they flee in terror. The powers will only acknowledge those in whom they see the wisdom of God as being the unswerving foundation of their lives. If the church itself lives by the wisdom of the world, then it has no effectual opposition to those powers.

> So that the manifold wisdom of God might *now* be made known [demonstrated] through the church.[7]

Though Paul wrote this letter two thousand years ago, the same demonstration to the powers needs presently to be made. The cosmic struggle is over which wisdom, or value system, or way of perceiving reality, is going to prevail. We know that the whole world lies in the power of Satan, who is also the father of lies. We need also to realize the degree to which these powers have been successful in deceiving mankind about truth, about reality, and about the purposes of life itself. They are enslaving mankind over things that are immediately visible before them

---

[7] Ephesians 3:10a. Emphasis mine.

and completely shut out any view of the things that pertain to eternity.

The powers are both enslaving and tyrannical, wanting to dominate mankind and God's creation. The first mandate to Adam was to take dominion over God's creation. Satan rules by control and domination. God's dominion has a very different character and rule. The former expresses the distinctive genius of the character of Satan, and the latter the character of God. Both are in contention for the triumphant possession and rule over creation.

THE WORLD AS SYSTEM

Scofield, the British theologian, defines *world* as the *present world system*, a system that is antithetical to God in every point and particular. The word *system* suggests something that man has made out of his own reason and ability. Even in the religious world, we are continually tempted to become a system, or to systematize something, and to bring it under human arrangement.

Institutions are not just objective organizations summoned by men to provide for human need. They have a life of their own, a purpose of their own, and a reason for being that seeks for its own perpetuation. If you begin to challenge their assumptions, and the premises by which they have their being, you begin to touch the powers that exist invisibly behind them. The same thing is true in the world of culture, human government and religion. In fact, there is no place where the powers have a more powerful influence than in religious institutions. Climbing up the ladder of religious success, with all of its honors and esteem, gives an open door to the powers to come in and find lodging.

In order to preserve its interests, the world's wisdom will resort to violence. On the other hand, the wisdom of God will give itself over to becoming the *victim* of violence. It will suffer violence against itself, as exemplified by the Lord Himself at the cross, rather than preserve itself by reacting with force.

The world as system enslaves mankind, whereby your whole life is spent in keeping your head above water. The system makes sure your time and your attention are completely distracted from God, so that you give yourself to the gods of this world. Are we, as God's people, willing to be radically other than what this present world is? Or, are we more comfortable with a place of acceptance and respect *in* the world and *in* its system, while, at the same time, trying to be a Christian in a Sunday manner of speaking?

> From the mouth of infants and nursing babes You have established strength because of Your adversaries, to make the enemy and the revengeful cease.[8]

God's adversaries celebrate fame, prestige, importance and the things that men admire. On the other hand, God's most significant work will be performed through men whom no one knows. Paul said of himself: "Unknown, yet well known." Unknown to men, but well known to God. The powers know those who have authority, those who have kept themselves from the spirit and wisdom of the world.

---

[8] Psalm 8:2

God has chosen the foolish and the weak thing to confound the wisdom of this world. He chooses those who live without the need to possess, who do not seek prestige, who do not need to be recognized or acknowledged. The guileless and the childlike manifest the wisdom that defeats the powers. A Christianity that becomes prestigious, dignified, acceptable and respectable is no longer apostolic.

THE THEOCRATIC CONTEXT

Though fiercely contested by the powers, God is going to establish His theocratic[9] rule over His creation. This is the context in which the great struggle and drama is being played out. The key to the establishment of the rule of God centers in the people Israel.[10] As a nation, Israel presently has no consciousness of these things, but the church must be conscious of it, or it will not understand why God must be so ruthless in His dealings with that nation. He needs to prepare Israel for its own place in the rule of God, because the theocratic rule must take place *with* that nation and *in* its own land: "For the law will go forth from Zion and the word of the LORD from Jerusalem."[11]

This scripture needs to be taken as a literal statement of fact. The powers know it better than the church, and therefore they constantly seek to exterminate that nation, whose survival and restoration

---

[9] Theocracy is the government of God
[10] For a broader understanding of this subject, see the author's book: *The Mystery of Israel and the Church.*
[11] Isaiah 2:3b

to their God ushers in the theocratic rule of God. The disciples said to Jesus, "Lord, is it at this time You are restoring the kingdom to Israel?"[12]

At least they asked the right question, but they saw it only in a narrow, nationalistic sense, not recognizing the universal significance of that kingdom. The time for the restoration of the kingdom was for a later time. In a nutshell, the church is God's instrument in bringing Israel *into* that restored place, which then releases the Lord and His coming as King, and the bringing forth of that government.

We need to begin to think in governmental terms. The government of God is more than bureaucracy; it has to do with order, but it has also to do with values, with justice, righteousness, equity, peace, mercy, compassion and love. The world governments know nothing of these things; they are predicated on power, advantage and ambition. But the government of God is life-giving; it brings sanity and wholeness to mankind.

> For I do not want you, brethren, to be uninformed of this mystery—so that you will not be wise in your own estimation—that a partial hardening has happened to Israel until the fullness of the Gentiles has come in; and so all Israel will be saved.[13]

Presently, God is being opposed by the angelic order that He Himself established. When the full number of Gentiles needed, both qualitatively and quantitatively, to replace that fallen order has been

---

[12] Acts 1:6b
[13] Romans 11:25-26a

obtained, then all Israel will be saved. The glorified church will then rule and reign instead of the powers, from the very same heavenly places, only this time not *contrary* to the purposes of God, but *for* the purposes of God. What a difference that will make! That is why we will need glorified bodies, and why Jesus said to Nathaniel: "You are impressed because I saw you sitting under the fig tree! I will show you a greater thing; namely, angels ascending and descending upon My throne in Jerusalem, ruling and reigning with Me from the heavenlies.[14] In other words, glorified saints will be moving back and forth in concert with God and with a restored Israel in the outworking of the millennial Kingdom, ministering the wisdom of God over the earth.

THE FINAL DEFEAT

> When He had disarmed the rulers and authorities, He made a public display of them, having triumphed over them through Him [Jesus].[15]

A permanent, enduring and eternal victory was won over the powers of the air; it was the triumph of God *over* Satan. The victory was established, but the final defeat must come through the church. The powers were disarmed, but they still exist, and continue to play a tremendous role in intimidating, threatening and manipulating individuals and nations. Every time the cross is proclaimed in authenticity and

---

[14] See John 1:47-51 (Paraphrased!)
[15] Colossians 2:15

power, their defeat is made more manifest. The power of the cross is revealed wherever there is obedience unto suffering, wherever there is a trust in God, rather than a trust in ourselves. Every time the suffering of a death to self is demonstrated, the power of the resurrection life is released, and the powers are required to flee.

Jesus' sacrifice was only made possible by the operation of God's own Spirit, who is the eternal Spirit, and who is Himself the Spirit of sacrifice. Every time that sacrifice is made by the Spirit in a believer, it is another demonstration of what was expressed at the cross; it is the demonstration of God Himself, what He is in Himself. When *He* is exhibited, the powers of the air flee, and when He is exhibited *through* His church, then Christ's victory is again shown forth.

Every time we cease from acting out of self-interest, it is an act on earth that verifies and substantiates that there is a God in heaven. The wellspring of what explains us, our essential life and conduct, how we act and do, is entirely to be understood on the basis of a God who is unseen. Our conduct is what demonstrates *Him*, who and what *He* is. A true witness is one who demonstrates the truth of an invisible God by what is exhibited in his obedient denial of self-interest. It is a demonstration that is possible only by those who have determined not to hold their lives as dear unto themselves. Who else would care that the eternal purpose of God is fulfilled, except those who love Him more than their own lives?

The Power of the Cross

There is a power in the cross; a triumph was won there that needs to be made manifest in every place through the presence and the proclamation of a believing church. Where the powers see *this* faith, *this* understanding, *this* proclamation and the realization of *this* victory by those who themselves are no longer bound in their wisdom, they know that their final vanquishing and defeat is at hand.

As long as we are a people who are fearful for our security, who tremble over the issue of our own finances, who model ourselves after the world, and use their techniques for obtaining funds, then we constitute no threat to these powers. We need *ourselves* to live joyfully free from the powers, free from fear, from anxiety, from seduction and manipulation. Wherever we calculate things to produce a certain result or response, we are guilty of manipulation. As long as we are moving in the very wisdom of the powers themselves, we constitute no witness against them.

If the chief weapon of the powers is to intimidate mankind through fear of death and the necessity to survive, then they are defeated by a church that is not afraid of death. Jesus had an absolute confidence that nothing could terminate His life before the purposes of the Father were fulfilled. We need to have exactly the same confidence. When the doctors of the law were interrogating Stephen, he did not know that his death would be the outcome, but when it came, even with its suddenness, there was no pleading. His face shone and radiated like an angel. It seemed such a tragic waste that his life should be cut short. Though the Lord took him abruptly, there was never any sense of misgiving in Stephen that there was some error being made. He saw the heavens open and Jesus standing at the right hand of the Father to receive him. He saw that his earthly purposes were now finished.

THE MEANING OF THE CROSS

The prevailing view of the crucifixion of Jesus on the cross is essentially one of atonement, whereby the death of Jesus fulfilled a requirement to satisfy the Father, and that Jesus died as a substitute for us and our sin. The atonement is understood merely on a level that removes the guilt of personal sin. There is very little being said about the cross as God's work in destroying the works of the Devil, and defeating the *power* of sin and death.

It makes a profound difference how we view what took place at the cross. If we see sin only as personal moral failure, a mistake that can be paid for by the sacrifice of Jesus to remove the guilt of it, then we have totally misunderstood the work of God at the cross. To think of the cross as the triumph of God brings a very different view with regard to our place in the purposes of God. But if we are thinking only personally and individually, then heaven for us is a place where we will go and enjoy an eternal vacation. If we are thinking of the triumph of God, then the heavenlies are a place we will come to occupy in a governmental capacity, ruling and reigning with Him in the establishment of His theocratic kingdom.

The view that sin is only a personal failure trivializes sin. It is a view that does not recognize the radical power of evil, requiring the very sacrifice of God in His Son to defeat it at the cross. In other words, the revelation of evil comes by seeing what it cost God to meet and defeat it. The enormity and magnitude of what was wrought at the cross in the crucifixion of Jesus is the most powerful provision given of God to glimpse the magnitude of the evil power of sin itself.

A humanistic interpretation of the atonement has its ground in the failure to see both the radical hostility of God toward evil and His judgment of it. It is a view whereby sin is not recognized for the evil that it is. Therefore, it is concerned essentially with the guilt of sin, which can be relieved by the propitiation that Jesus provided in satisfying the need of the Father for a just retribution. It makes God the Father look like a heavy-handed Old Testament deity who demands a certain kind of justice to make the thing right, and that Jesus was that necessary "sacrifice."

This interpretation does not see that God was in Christ reconciling the world to Himself, but rather that Jesus the man, the perfect man, was the satisfaction that requited the Father's need for justice; that He was appeased as the God of vengeance and judgment. Consequently, our entire view of God will be negatively affected. It will be limited and inadequate, and our life and conduct will be much more sentimental and consoling to the flesh.

Jesus allowed Himself to suffer the full brunt of the wisdom of the powers of the air. But He was raised from that death by the power of the Father. There was a triumph over death and evil in the humility, meekness, long-suffering and patience of the

Lord. This is the true meaning of the cross. There are purposes in the atonement that go far beyond the benefit that comes to us as individuals. It is not that we are absolved of individual responsibility for sin, but that we need to see that our sins are related to the *power of sin*. The power of sin itself was defeated at the cross, and therefore we no longer need to live in it, or yield our members to it. New life is imparted; a new principle of life comes with the resurrection from that death.

The powers rubbed their hands in glee when they had Jesus totally in their power, but He went to His death as silent as a lamb, never once resisting them, but yielding Himself to that terrible power of darkness. It was by *that* ability to yield that Jesus triumphed over them. It was a final showdown, a conflict between two wisdoms; it was violent force and power in vicious brutality against the Lamb of God, slain from before the foundation of the world, who suffered in meekness and humility. The worst that could be brought *against* Him revealed the best that was *in* Him. Utter malice met utter magnanimity. The powers were made an open and public display. They were ridiculed by the very submitting of Jesus to the worst fury and vengeance, animosity and violence that they knew. The Lord did not react in kind, He did not shriek out, He did not plead for his life. Hell in all of its fury met Heaven in all of its humility, meekness and long-suffering. Heaven triumphed completely. Jesus bruised the head of the Serpent, but it is left to the church to make an eternal demonstration of the manifold wisdom of God, not just in this age, but in the ages to come.

The Provision of God in Fellowship

To be a people who demonstrate the wisdom of God, we will need the prayer and encouragement of those with a like mind and heart. The separation from the world is so painful, and its influence is so pervasive and powerful. We need the wisdom and counsel of others to maintain that freedom without again being sucked back into the power of the world. We will need to exhort one another daily. We will need to be in close attendance of one another in an environment conducive to correction and reproof, because the leaven of sin will find its way in, and we can be drawn back into the world.

In the intensity of life together, and in that inter-relationship, we can more easily recognize the early signs of sin from which we need to separate ourselves. How do we discern the things that are evil when they are depicted and set before us as being something not only innocent, but beneficial, pleasant and good to have and to enjoy? It is going to take an uncommon ability to see through the appearance of something, and to recognize the inherent evil that is in it. The issue of discernment is not a magical ability, but relative to the authentic spirituality of an entire fellowship. Our discerning will either be dull, or acute, based on the quality of our corporate life, integrity and truth.

This is calling for a church that is a people who are *together*, whose corporate intercession compels the powers of the air to flee. It is inevitable that such a knit of life will be resisted, and that the powers themselves will test it, and resort even to oppression and persecution. We can almost gauge with accuracy how much of a threat we represent to the powers by the degree of opposition and persecution we receive; the lack of it being the evidence that we are not yet the church we ought to be!

In the book of Acts, we read of those who did not think that the things they possessed were their own. It is a profound statement of the depth of the sanctifying work of God that had broken men loose from their deep selfishness. They were brought to a configuration and quality of relationship that was the particular distinctive of the church. It was a quality of life of which the world knew nothing. They were a demonstration on the earth of what God's essential relationship is in heaven, and the particular character by which He relates with Himself in His triune composition as the Godhead. It is a relationship of an unusual self-giving quality by which the one exalts the other and defers to the other.

The genius of the Godhead Himself had come to earth, and was now being demonstrated by Jews, famous for their selfishness and contention. A fellowship that comes together merely for services as a conglomerate of individualities is no threat to the powers. They only recognize an authenticity that is a reflection of what is in the Godhead Himself.

As the church, our call to resist the Devil is not dependent upon what we *do*, but what we *are*. It is something in the *character* of the church. Our victory will be related to the quality and consistent character of the fellowship itself. If there is any condescension to the wisdom of the powers, through concern for one's life and security, then the powers have a place of penetration. When they see a people who are resolute in their faith, who know that their security does not come from their employer or business, but from God, then the powers are held in check.

THE POWER OF TRUE PRAISE

Do not be fooled to think that the euphoric feeling we enjoy by our music and choruses is really the statement of a vibrant faith in God. *We* may enjoy it, and we *hope* that God is being blessed also, but we need to be ruthlessly honest and gird ourselves with truth—especially the truth about our own condition. The issue is not whether our worship pleases us or facilitates the service, but whether it is in fact true worship. Is it the spontaneous expression of the redemptive work of God that has been experienced in our lives authentically and corporately?

Loudness is power, and when the sound amplifiers are turned up, it can become a manipulation, often predicated on the notion that the powers will be defeated through militant or revved up music labeled as "worship." The moment we begin to employ worship for purposes other than worship, it is no longer true worship. God knows when there is a worship that has no strings attached. True worship is the adoration and devotion that God deserves because He is God. But when we make of it a manipulation and a tool toward an end, even a religiously desired end, then it is no longer worship. We are on the enemy's ground, employing an expediency to obtain an end.

"Jesus we know and Paul we know, but who are

you?" may well be asked of us by the powers. "Yes, we hear your praise, and we hear your choruses, but there is something about them that is hollow. It is merely singing, and it is not, therefore, something that we are required to acknowledge." This is what the powers utter when they encounter a fellowship operating in less than the fullness of its inheritance in Christ. There is a praise and worship that is mere singing, but there is also a praise that wells up to heaven, which is more than the product of charismatic manipulation. It is a praise that is a spontaneous breaking forth in celebration of the God who has saved us, not only out of fear, insecurity and anxiety, but who has brought us to a transcendent place of apostolic faith. That kind of praise devastates the powers of darkness.

Paul and Silas' imprisonment in Acts 16 is a superb demonstration of the wisdom of God. At midnight they were praying and singing praises to God because they believed that their present suffering was the very consequence of their obedience. Even though only one woman was affected by their ministry, they were in the place of obedience to the heavenly vision. It did not matter whether they would live or die; that was not the issue. They had a deep faith in the sovereignty of God. They were privileged to share in His sufferings, and their rejoicing and praise was an expression of that.

Praise in the midst of adversity and suffering is the overwhelming evidence of the reality of the invisible God. It contradicts the wisdom of the powers, who say that when you are suffering, you are supposed to pout, feel sorry for yourself, and blame God or man. But when we can praise God in the midst of our sufferings, it is a wisdom that defeats the powers, and they are required to flee. Jesus endured all of His suffering for the *joy* that was set before Him, in the anticipation of what would be the consequence of His suffering for eternity. This is the wisdom of God, because rejoicing in suffering is a contradiction. It is contrary to reason and everything we think natural to man. It is the greater wisdom, but it is not enough just to speak it. It has got to be made manifest by a church whose inner life is itself the proclamation of God's manifold wisdom.

THE MANIFOLD WISDOM OF GOD

If we have any intention of becoming an authentic expression of God's people upon the earth, we will incite the persecution of these powers. There is a particular cruelty and hatred in mankind that expresses itself against God and His people whenever opportunity allows. In those moments, to love and pray for our persecutors is demonstrating the wisdom of God. When Stephen forgave those who were taking his life, the eternal power of that statement broke into the consciousness of Saul, one of the principal persecutors of the early church. Something happens when meekness and humility meet utter viciousness. The very nature of God, revealed under supreme duress and pressure, is a demonstration of the wisdom of God that the powers are obliged to recognize.

Jesus did not strive to preserve His own bodily life. He *yielded* up His spirit, uttering the words: "Father, forgive them." Those words were heard by a

Roman centurion, a Gentile man. He had likely seen many victims of crucifixion squirm and curse as they died, for they were only mere men clutching at their lives. But when he saw *this* God-man die magnificently under extreme duress and pain, words broke forth out of his mouth: "Truly, this was the Son of God!" He was compelled to recognize the true identity of Jesus by what was exhibited in His ultimate suffering unto death,. That identity would not have been revealed *except* at the cross in a suffering unto death as being the ultimate demonstration of the testimony of who Jesus is.

As Jesus walked, so also are we to walk in this world. We say we serve Him and love Him, but in the conduct of our daily lives, how much do we consistently subscribe to another wisdom and way? Manipulation, teasing and flattery are ways that we seek to bend the will of another, and are therefore evil. Every time we employ the wisdom of this world, we bow to and serve its gods.

How do we react under duress now? Our little impatient moods, our critical spirits and our irritation with one another are already evidence of how little prepared we are for the cosmic struggle before us. The trials and irritations that come to us are the provision of God for the shaping of His character in us. God wants to move us to that ultimate place of response, that when persecution comes, we shall stand graciously and exhibit His wisdom. Then shall we demonstrate the triumph of the cross, and by the eternal Spirit, we shall offer ourselves up, as Jesus did in that final moment. The eternal Spirit was offering up God Himself, so that in the moment of His trial and suffering, the demonstration that was being made to the powers was the demonstration of God being *all in all*, and bringing to the core of the cosmos His very essence and being.

When that same demonstration comes from the church, the triumph is again made known, and the powers demolished. This is the eternal purpose of God for the church. To be crucified with Christ needs to be the very basis for our overcoming. For once we have experienced *that* death, and risen to newness of life, of what then shall we be afraid? This is a call to maturity, for a church to come into its fullness, according to the eternal purpose of God, for which He has created all things. May we *see* our calling, and rise up to meet it, and receive every difficulty, trial and experience that comes into our life as from God's hand. This will give us a new perspective on the role of suffering, and a much more realistic anticipation of our future persecution.

The Overcoming of the Saints

It takes an episode out of the life of David to show the ages-long conflict of wisdoms. It is unlikely that David was aware of the significance of his act toward Saul, but *what* he did, and *how* he acted, in a particular moment, affected the whole subsequent character of the kingdom. The *coming* kingdom has a particular character that God is not ashamed to call "Davidic."

King Saul is in relentless pursuit of David's life.[16] The conflict between them is a picture of the enmity

---

[16] See 1 Samuel 24

between what these men represented in themselves. Saul stands for something visible and external, prestigious and impressive, both religiously and politically. He had all of the externalities and outward credentials of what we think a king should be. He was a convenience that God allowed Israel because they wanted a human king to rule over them, though God Himself was their King.

When God told Saul to destroy the Amalekite men, women, children and animals, he did *not* do it. He was partial in his obedience, and saved the best of the sheep and oxen for a sacrifice unto the Lord. He could not bring himself to slay Agag, king of the Amalekites. It was the prophet Samuel who wept all through the night at Saul's disobedience, and who himself then took a sword and hacked Agag to pieces. Though Saul could not bring himself to a complete obedience by slaying the historical enemies of God, he later destroyed the whole city of Nob, a priestly community. He exterminated an entire community because they had helped David in his flight.

David, on the other hand, is the insignificant, plain individual, who had recently feigned madness, and who now finds himself in a cave in flight from Saul. Nothing has changed. The institutional, religious systems will always bitterly oppose the Davidic people of God. The "kingly" person that men tend to celebrate cannot tolerate the life of the seemingly insignificant one who sees himself as but a flea. It is a timeless, classic contest. The true people of God will be harried and pursued by those who cannot abide their very existence.

What is it about David that so infuriated Saul?

Why should a helpless and insignificant young man so antagonize a man of power and religious and political authority? What kind of threat could he have conceivably constituted for Saul? To be weak, foolish and dependent upon God are exactly what infuriate a people who are religious, but who establish their religious proficiency on the basis of their own self-confident ability, and what *they* have raised up, and what *they* can do. In weakness and inoffensiveness, David represented a threat, not only to Saul, but especially to the powers.

A critical moment came in David's life. He performed something in the character of God that distinguished the wisdom of God from the wisdom of the powers. God's ends can *only* be obtained by God's means, and His means must be consistent with His character. We cannot take or establish God's kingdom if it is not in keeping with the character of God Himself. If we use manipulation in altar calls by playing on emotions, or getting people to come forward by some kind of psycho-spiritual manipulation, then its activity is not in keeping with the character of the kingdom.

What we are, having been formed at the hand of God, comes to bear in the moment of crisis, and this is the moment that came to David. Saul came into the cave where David was hiding, and David's men said to him:

> "Behold, this is the day of which the LORD said to you, 'Behold; I am about to give your enemy into your hand, and you shall

do to him as it seems good to you.' "[17]

His men expected that David would kill his persecutor, thereby getting rid of the nuisance. It was a critical moment for David, and he was totally free to do what he would choose to do. What we are, and what we choose to do when we are free to choose what we will, and what we choose to think when we are free to think what we will, is in fact what we are. It is what we do in our freedom that is a testimony to the powers of darkness.

Instead of taking Saul's life, David cut off the edge of Saul's robe, and it came about afterward that his conscience bothered him for doing that act. If you want a glimpse into the heart of David, and the character of David, it is precisely to be found here. David was sensitive in his conscience, and the very cutting of Saul's robe troubled him. What kind of a man is this?

> Far be it from me because of the LORD that I should do this thing to my lord, the LORD's anointed, to stretch out my hand against him, since he is the LORD's anointed.[18]

David is describing an apostate and backslidden king, who is soon to suffer his own destruction. Everything about Saul is contemptible, and yet David respects him, not because of his conduct, but because of his *office*. In so doing, David respects the Lord, whose anointing once came upon that man. It is a respect for authority that does not take into account

---

[17] 1 Samuel 24:4
[18] 1 Samuel 24:6b

how Saul failed. A respect for the office is a respect and honoring of the God who originally gave it. Has the church given to Israel, though Israel is backslidden and apostate, the measure of respect for what its place once was in God?

> David persuaded his men with these words and did not allow them to rise up against Saul. And Saul arose, left the cave, and went on his way.[19]

What was Saul's way? The way of a murderer; the way of a cold-hearted man bent on the destruction of that which he sees as a threat to his kingdom. To allow Saul to leave was to invite ongoing persecution for David. It is clear that Saul's tears were "crocodile" tears:

> "You are more righteous than I; for you have dealt well with me, while I have dealt wickedly with you. You have declared today that you have done good to me, that the LORD delivered me into your hand and yet you did not kill me. For if a man finds his enemy, will he let him go away safely? May the LORD therefore reward you with good in return for what you have done to me this day.[20]

It is only a matter of time before those tears dry up, and Saul again pursues and hunts down David to end his life. And because of this, David's act was an act of righteousness. Is righteousness truly righteousness if it does not cost us anything, and does not

---

[19] Ibid., v.7
[20] Ibid., vv.17b-19

involve a threat to the preservation of our life? The garments that clothe the saints of the last days are their righteous deeds. David would not condescend to a convenience that would preserve his life. He would not stretch forth his arm; he would not employ a means to obtain an end. David's faith was to let God judge and vindicate. We need to remember that David was a man of war. He could be ruthless when he had to, but here he would not stretch forth his arm to save his own life.

We must not miss this statement that David makes:
> After whom has the king of Israel come out? Whom are you pursuing? A dead dog, a single flea?[21]

David is not playing on words here. The fact that he is a man of war, and *still* refuses to stretch forth his hand to kill when he has someone defenseless, is all the more a profound statement of the character of God and His kingdom. David is a man who really thinks that he is a dead dog and a flea. He did not see anything about himself that was worth preserving. Therefore, he did not hold his life as dear unto himself. If God was more glorified by his death than by his continuing to live, then so be it. Our basic error is that we think we have a right to preserve the creaturely thing that we are. David was "dead and hid with God in Christ;" he was a man brought back from the dead, through the resurrection of Jesus Christ, no longer to live for himself, but for *Him*. Are we more like Saul or more like David? Do we perform the expedient thing?

---

[21] Ibid., v.14

Do we pursue our own interests? Do we rise up against the thing that threatens us?

David calls out to the astonished Saul:

> May the LORD judge between you and me, and may the LORD avenge me on you; but my hand shall not be against you."[22]

The confidence that David exhibits is more than bravado. It is predicated on a deep knowledge of God and a trust in His sovereignty; that even if God should allow him to be Saul's victim, then so be it. It is a faith of an ultimate kind, allowing our persecutors to be free to come back and repeat what has always been their intention.

The whole future of the kingdom was hanging on *that* moment, and more than that, a descendent from David's own loins would one day be the Messiah of all mankind. If David was cut off, then that line would be cut off, and the whole Messianic succession destroyed. David could have said, "Listen, I am called to be the king of Israel. A descendant of mine will not only be a King forever but also the salvation of all mankind. When I see the intention of God for my life, then it has *got* to be preserved." David, however, would *not* say that, for he knew that if God would not preserve what pertains to Him, then he himself would not do it by stretching out his hand.

Our attitude toward religious institutions, governments and any kind of defunct authority will be critical in manifesting the wisdom of God. If the enemy can bring us onto his ground, where we would rail against something, or complain, or be

---
[22] Ibid., v.12

contemptuous, or critical in an ungodly way, then they have won the game. Our attitude in our hearts is where the struggle and conflict is decided.

> But Michael the archangel, when he disputed with the devil and argued about the body of Moses, did not dare pronounce against him a railing judgment, but said, "The Lord rebuke you!"[23]

One of the dangerous things taking place now in the church is the kind of religious egotism that says: "It is up to us to put the Devil in his place." Be careful, because we are cautioned not to rail against the Devil and his angels. Though they are a fallen, angelic order, they were once given governmental position to administer the purposes of God.

While Jesus was hanging on the cross, He was railed at with jeers and taunts. If anything is calculated to vex a man, it is that the people for whom you came do not even recognize or appreciate it. Furthermore, they are tormenting you verbally in your anguish and suffering. Jesus was silent. The crisis revealed what was in Him, and what was in Him was the character of God in patient forbearance, in suffering, in mercy and forgiveness. The Son revealed the Father.

David even calls Saul his father: "Now, my father, see! Indeed, see the edge of your robe in my hand!"[24] David had a son's respect for an older man as a father, though the man was anything but a good father. He failed in every category, but from David's point of view, Saul was his father. David's respect for Saul is

---

[23] Jude 1:9
[24] Ibid., v.11a

contrary to the wisdom of this age, the wisdom by which the world lives its life. When nothing else will work, men will stretch forth their hands in violence, and they will justify it in order to obtain their ends. In the last analysis, you can know the true faith because it will never resort to violence to obtain its ends. Any religion that purports to be of God, and requires violence to obtain its ends, is by its very demonstration necessarily false.

How many of us see divorce as violence? It is a tearing of a relationship asunder. If our spouse is an irritant to us, or counterproductive, or opposes us, then we think that we can justify the violence of divorce. Few have faulted us for so doing, and with scant interruption, we continue "our important service" with a new and more attractive spouse! As time goes on, few will remember that there was once another spouse. The eternal purpose of God suffers a setback, because we have condescended to the wisdom of the world in what was expedient for our satisfaction.

David demonstrated the meekness of the Davidic kingdom. It is the willingness to allow one's life to be expended rather than to save it.

Daniel writes of a "horn" that was "waging war with the saints and overpowering them."[25] The Book of Revelation compounds the mystery yet more by adding: "It was also given to him [the Beast] to make war with the saints and to overcome them."[26] How mind-boggling to consider that God allows His enemies to devastate His people, so as to overcome them. Where then is the victory of the saints? It seems

---

[25] Daniel 7:21b
[26] Revelation 13:7a

like a contradiction; so how, then, are overcomers victorious? But what if the "overcoming" is in the *dying?* It then becomes the issue of *how* we die. In allowing ourselves to be overcome, we demonstrate the wisdom of God that defeats the powers. In other words, we *overcome* in being overcome.

When Jesus overturned the moneychangers' tables, that act of violence was more against property than against men. He overturned the tables, but He did not overturn men. It was an act of meekness, though it was violent in its character. It came in the moment of God's own choosing in order to validate the Messianic claim of Jesus in His jealousy for the Father's house. If God requires you to act in that kind of vehemence in the moment of His choosing, then to *not* do that would be disobedient. To submit is to be meek, all the more if it is contrary to your own disposition.

Conclusion

Stephen's martyrdom had repercussions that he knew nothing about; namely, the conversion of Saul of Tarsus. There was something in Stephen's death that haunted Saul. He had never seen a man die more gloriously, or show more graciousness toward his executors. Mere religion cannot produce that witness. It took a demonstration of the character of God in Stephen, a man who was so below Saul's own prestigious status. When God reveals His character in the weak and undistinguished vessel to a man of such prestige, it is a devastating revelation of God. Could Saul have been converted with anything less than a demonstration before him of the supreme triumph of the wisdom of God?

God did not think that the sacrifice of Stephen was too extravagant to bring about the salvation of Saul, who later became the chief apostle to the church. The Gentile church will be called upon to be a martyr-people, like Stephen, as a final demonstration to a Jewish, Saul-like nation, who cannot be saved on any other ground less than this same demonstration.[27]

Stephen gave his persecutors a long history of Israel, and then he came to the final climax: "Behold, I see the heavens opened up and the Son of Man standing at the right hand of God."[28] He saw the Son of Man in the presence of God, in the place of authority, which meant the end of the false authority that his persecutors had established in their own religious institutions. When they heard *that*, Stephen was finished. The powers of darkness resident in them rose up with such a fury. They were the same ones who sent Jesus to His crucifixion. It was the same fury, but now ventilated against Stephen, whose face shone like an angel.

This age will end with a church of the same character as was demonstrated by Jesus, Stephen and David, whose acts revealed a greater wisdom, a righteousness greater than what the Pharisees could exhibit. It was not the righteousness of impeccably maintained principles, but a righteousness that forfeits one's own life. This alone demonstrates the very nature of God, thus revealing the wisdom and glory of God.

---

[27] See Author's book: *The Mystery of Israel and the Church*
[28] Acts 7:56b

We may have a right to contend as sufferers of injustice and oppression, but there is a wisdom and a greater power revealed in not contending. It is an ultimate expression of trust in God. In this way, the false wisdom is revealed as false, and its captives are set free. This is true liberation. Wherever there is a congregation freed from the false wisdom of the powers, consistently and unselfconsciously displayed, there the kingdom of God is also revealed.

CHAPTER 4

Apostolic Proclamation

The first statement of the anointed ministry of Jesus took place in a synagogue, in the reading of a portion of Isaiah 61: "The Spirit of the Lord is upon Me because He anointed Me to preach."[1] There is a connection between anointing and true preaching. The preached or proclaimed word has a particular quality that distinguishes it from any other kind of speaking or oratory. True preaching is a remarkable phenomenon, even a matter of life and death because:

> How then will they call on Him in whom they have not believed? How will they believe in Him whom they have not heard? And how will they hear without a preacher? How will they preach unless they are sent?[2]

---

[1] See Luke 4:18
[2] Romans 10:14-15a

Preaching, by one who is sent, is at the heart of the mission calling of the church to the unbelieving world. Those whom God sends are given the Spirit without measure. This sending is therefore critical, for which reason God establishes local fellowships of believers—we have to be sent from *somewhere*.

Preaching the word of God is much more than bringing a word that is biblically correct; it is more than the correct formulation of the doctrines of God. The word of God is a divine communication of a uniquely powerful kind, all the more remarkable in that God intends it to be expressed through a human vessel. Therefore, we need a deep appreciation for the holy sacrament of preaching. Paul's own acute awareness of the phenomenon is revealed in his first epistle to the Thessalonians:

> For this reason we also constantly thank God that when you received the word of God which you heard from us, you accepted it not as the word of men, but for what it really is, the word of God, which also performs its work in you who believe.[3]

We need to read this as a literal and accurate description of a particular mode of speaking that is rare in our own time. If what makes this communication distinctive is its power to perform a work, what then is its character? Believers, and particularly ministers, are forever seeking to establish their reputations and their acceptance on some basis other than the preached word. There are many who make careers out of their ability to speak. They have a facility with words and a corresponding gift to communicate them. If one is attractive, winsome with an audience, one can go far in the religious world. However, true preaching bypasses

---

[3] 1 Thessalonians 2:13

all natural talents; it is altogether a divine and supernatural phenomenon. It is the word of *life*. It quickens the *dead*. It sets in motion things that have a myriad of consequences. It is a word that is *sent*.

Ironically, this kind of speaking has to find expression through the mouth of an earthen vessel rather than directly from God Himself. Though the word comes out of the mouth of a human vessel, its origin is divine and heavenly. The speaker participates in the process; the Lord employs the man's personality, his accent, his disposition and his heart. It is the bringing together of an overwhelming contradiction, and where this phenomenon is at work, it is nothing less than an excruciating suffering for the one who is speaking. Every time he speaks, it is the same trembling, the same uncertainty, and the same deep sense of the patent impossibility of the task.

Preaching is a struggle, an ultimate challenge every time it is undertaken. We can make many good biblical statements, but that is not the same as communicating the word *as* God's word. The first communicates mere biblical knowledge, but the latter has the power to constitute an "event" for the hearers. My own observation is that more than ninety-five percent of all Christian preaching and teaching is speaking *about* God, or making biblical statements that are interesting and insightful, but which do not constitute the expression of the word *as* God's word. It is not true preaching, and the evidence is that the hearers remain unchanged. They are not going from faith to faith, or from glory to glory, because the "event" of preaching has not been put before them.

The whole church needs to have a higher standard

set before it than what it presently understands about preaching. We dare not come up to the platform, open the Bible, clear our throats, call the congregation to attention, say a prayer, open our mouths and commence, without a terrible sense of foreboding of the great weight that falls upon *that* moment. If it is *not* the word of God, there will be a form of death going forth, instead of life. There is no neutrality in the kingdom. Either the word is going to enliven, or it will bring numbness and dullness in the hearing of it.

THE WORD OF THE CROSS

> For the word of the cross is foolishness to those who are perishing, but to us who are being saved it is the power of God.[4]
>
> For since in the wisdom of God the world through its wisdom did not come to know God, God was well-pleased through the foolishness of the message preached to save those who believe.[5]

The word of the cross *is* the power of God; it contains an inherent, divinely penetrating ability to register divine truths *despite* the severest religious, cultural and ethnic resistance; it has an ability to create faith in the hearers, causing them to believe unto salvation. It performs a work in them that believe, or a work that brings one to the place of believing. It is a heavenly word proclaimed in the earth, not only to those who may be willing hearers, but also, and just as much, to those who are resistant hearers. Earth resists

---

[4] 1 Corinthians 1:18
[5] Ibid., v.21

heaven, and every power of darkness wants to cloud the minds of men and keep them from understanding and responding. Therefore, a word of an ultimate kind is needed, like a hammer on a rock, to break that resistance.

The word of the cross does not mean that the cross itself is necessarily the subject matter. The substance of the crucifixion event, replicated in the humiliation of the preaching, is the re-enactment of the cross-experience itself. Every time the cross is re-enacted in any humiliation that comes from an act of obedience, the power that was demonstrated at the cross is again given opportunity to be expressed.

The reason we see so little of the power of God in preaching is that men take pains to avoid the humiliation of the cross, preferring to play it safe with man-deferring sermons. There is an unwillingness to take the risk of failure and to trust God for the word *in that moment*. There is a genuine place for sermon preparation, but in the preaching event itself, room must be made for God. If we insulate ourselves from God by our own religious, human and professional preparation, we void the cross and the foolishness of it, namely, the suffering and the humiliation, and therefore rob the cross of its power. No matter what might be a man's natural qualifications and strengths, he must, in that tremulous moment, be in weakness and much trembling.

A preacher, who intentionally empties himself in the dying to his own ability to speak, trusting rather for the word of God to be given, will experience a measure of suffering akin to that of the crucified Christ. He becomes foolish in a humiliation unto death. This is at the heart of all true speaking. The man speaking sees to it that his own ability will not be his dependency or source of supply. God does not want the faith of men to be established on human eloquence, but only on the basis of the power of God.

The preaching that is the power of God comes when a man abandons himself, when he refuses to lean on his own expertise, his own savvy, or his gift of the gab. Pulling out *that* plug is the death. It is something one can never get used to, but is to be tasted again and again. Every occasion is as terrifying and mortifying as if you had never done it before. It is a recurring experience in death. Who is willing to taste those kinds of deaths? Who is willing to abandon his own proven and trusted ability and confidence, and trust that the same power that raised Jesus from the dead will now raise the speaker and his message?

The issue is the issue of the cross, and the word of God will not come to men with full conviction, except through the lips of those who know the cross in their own experience, and are willing to suffer the humiliation of it again and again in the very foolishness of their speaking. If our speaking is not foolishness, then it is not a true speaking. It may amuse men, it may even inform them, but it will *never* be an event.

To preach truly is not the issue of skill or learned technique, but a divine mystery. The very word "preaching" is derived from the Latin word *praedikare*, which means "to make known." Whenever Christ's humiliation is explicated in the foolishness of preaching, He is again revealed and set forth to be the Savior. For just as God gives grace to the humble, so does He, who is full of grace and truth, have opportunity to intersect time and eternity, heaven and earth, in the moment of authentic meekness when a preacher ceases from himself.

A familiar illustration of this cruciform life is to be found in Paul's first letter to the Corinthians where he writes:

> And when I came to you, brethren, I did not come with superiority of speech or of wisdom, proclaiming to you the testimony of God. For I determined to know nothing among you except Jesus Christ, and Him crucified.[6]

For all of Paul's erudition and religious knowledge, this kind of self-imposed limitation required a painful determination. The trouble is that we know so much, and so much that we know wants to find expression. Therefore, it requires a determination to put away what is so accessible and available to our preaching.

God will not give His glory to another, except when it is exclusively *Himself* being expressed by the preacher. How many of us are willing to live on that razor's edge? How many of us are not so much concerned with the glory of God as we are in seeking to avoid the embarrassment of failure? That is why we have so little resurrection-event in our weekly pulpit preaching. That is why safe, conventional preaching can never be an event in God. As someone has said, and I believe it out of my own experience, "Every true preaching is a raising again of the dead." We need to have an enhanced appreciation for what resurrection means as a God-event in the spoken word. We will never be a mouthpiece for God if we are trying to preserve our reputation, or if we are afraid ourselves to experience death.

The man who loves to talk, who loves to be public, who enjoys being seen and heard, will never

---

[6] 1 Corinthians 2:1-2

speak the word of event. The man who sighs and groans when he gets up to the pulpit, and would rather that the floor open up and swallow him, who does not want to be there, who feels terribly uncomfortable, and who knows that he is not going to be understood, is the man out of whose mouth the word of true preaching is most likely to come. Like Jonah, who wanted to escape the call of God, the man who does not want to preach is the only one qualified to preach.

With so many of God's people content with mere scriptural or doctrinal correctness, it is urgent to elevate the church's level of regard and expectation for the word as a creative event, producing change and establishing faith in the hearer, a word beyond what is merely informational. It is the *word* that is the event, not the stylistic presentation.

Where that creative word is not expressed, the sermon stands in jeopardy of becoming mere ceremony, a piece of familiar and unchallenging predictability, requiring nothing from its hearers and making no demand. It may fill the space that has been allocated for it, but there is no glory in the church; we have only been sermonized. To that measure, we are incapacitated as God's witnesses in the world, and constitute only a sleepy, Sunday religious culture that the world can well afford to ignore.

How out of tune our contemporary preaching is to the whole tenor of Paul's exhortation to Timothy: "Preach the word; be ready in season and out of season; reprove, rebuke, exhort, with great patience and instruction."[7] Evidently, to preach the word was to be particular, pointed and uncompromising in confronting the brethren on the condition of their lives and the necessity for change.

---

[7] 2 Timothy 4:2

In our age, degrees and credentials from institutions carry more weight than being authentically and apostolically charged for the call of ministry. This is only a symptom of the yet larger sickness, namely, the substitution of the glory of God in the church for a man-pleasing *ethos*. That is why we have such shallow teaching and preaching. God is not giving His authority and depth to men who would use and usurp it for their own ends, for their own names and for their religious success.

True Preaching Waits on True Sending

Given the absence of deep conversions effected by the preaching of the word in our own generation, one wonders if we have sufficiently considered the meaning of the word "sent." Have we naïvely assumed that *any* promulgation of the gospel is blessed and honored of God? If preaching Christ is more than the message *about* Him, but rather the showing forth *of* Him, then the God who sends may yet be waiting for suitable candidates for His sending.

Everything rests on the man being *sent*. This means that those in the fellowship who are sending him are of one mind with him. They necessarily share the same mentality and cross-centeredness, or God would not say, "Set apart for Me." To be sent is much more than being commissioned; it is to be sent in the place of another. The Other is Christ Himself; it is through those who are sent that the people hear Christ's voice and speech:

> But what does it say? "THE WORD IS NEAR YOU, IN YOUR MOUTH AND IN YOUR HEART," that is, the word of faith which we are preaching, that if you confess

with your mouth Jesus as Lord and believe in your heart that God raised Him from the dead, you will be saved; for with the heart a person believes, resulting in righteousness, and with the mouth he confesses, resulting in salvation. For the Scripture says, "WHOEVER BELIEVES IN HIM WILL NOT BE DISAPPOINTED." For there is no distinction between Jew and Greek; for the same Lord is Lord of all, abounding in riches for all who call upon Him; for "WHOEVER WILL CALL ON THE NAME OF THE LORD WILL BE SAVED." How then will they call on Him in whom they have not believed? How will they believe in Him whom they have not heard? And how will they hear without a preacher? How will they preach unless they are sent? Just as it is written, "HOW BEAUTIFUL ARE THE FEET OF THOSE WHO BRING GOOD NEWS OF GOOD THINGS!" However, they did not all heed the good news; for Isaiah says, "LORD, WHO HAS BELIEVED OUR REPORT? So faith comes from hearing, and hearing by the word of Christ."[8]

Much of modern-day evangelism has reduced the gospel to a simple formula, an "easy-believism" that has left many outside the kingdom. The hearers recite a repeat-after-me prayer, thus missing the whole profound point. There is a certain kind of hearing that is needed for a certain kind of believing. Paul quotes from the Book of Isaiah where the prophet says:

---

[8] Romans 10:8-17

> Therefore My people shall know My name;
> therefore in that day I am the one who is
> speaking, "Here I am."
>
> How lovely on the mountains are the feet of
> him who brings good news, who announces
> peace and brings good news of happiness,
> who announces salvation, and says to Zion,
> "Your God reigns!"[9]

The word "announce" is better understood as meaning "pronounce" or "proclaim." It is more than an announcement of information; it is a creative word of God, a *rhema* word, in the hearing of which an event occurs, and faith is established where there was none before.

To propound the faith to others in a systematic way by which their reason can be satisfied, so that they can be won over by some kind of invincible logic of statements, is not the basis by which God desires to reveal Himself. The key to believing and to calling on the name of the Lord is the hearing of a particular word, namely, the word of Christ Himself: "I am the one who is speaking. Here I am." The feet of those who bear good news are called lovely, or blessed, because God is the One who is speaking. He has full possession of that earthen vessel, and therefore it is actually Christ's *own* word. They hear the voice of God, and His word is as creative as it was in the beginning when He spoke and the world came into being.

In other words, the voice, the speaking, the content and the words that constitute the creative event that establishes faith to believe, enabling the hostile and resistant to call on God's name, is actually God's voice and His speaking. We might believe it could

---

[9] Isaiah 52:6-7

come through a giant of the faith like Paul, but can we believe for the phenomenon to come through ourselves? Does God have enough possession of us that we might say with absolute certitude: "It is He who is speaking, here He is"?

How shall they believe that Jesus was raised from the dead except that the evidence of the resurrection is in the words, the demeanor, the voice and the disposition of the one who stands before them? How can they believe unless they see the truth of the resurrection in those who bring the word? Nothing less will bring about the salvation of the unsaved—particularly the unsaved Jew in the last days.

RESURRECTION LIFE

The issue of the resurrection is inextricably linked to the authenticity of the lordship of Jesus in the believer's life.

> Being found in appearance as a man, He humbled Himself by becoming obedient to the point of death, even death on a cross. For this reason also, God highly exalted Him, and bestowed on Him the name which is above every name, so that at the name of Jesus EVERY KNEE WILL BOW, of those who are in heaven and on earth and under the earth, and that every tongue will confess that Jesus Christ is Lord, to the glory of God the Father.[10]

The resurrection of Jesus is the exaltation of the One who experienced an ultimate humiliation unto death. In other words, because of His obedience unto

---

[10] Philippians 2:8-11

death, He was raised; and that resurrection exalts Him above every name as Lord. That is why "whosoever confesses that Jesus is Lord and believes in their heart that God has raised Him from the dead shall be saved."[11] Lordship and resurrection are inextricably joined together.

In seeing the evidence of the resurrection of Christ in the messenger, and hearing the voice of the resurrected Christ, the unbeliever, who has had no preparation for this encounter, is faced with the end of the lordship over *his* own life; he will no longer determine what he is going to do with his life. When Jesus becomes Lord, our self-will and self-determination end, and God says, "Now you'll do *My* bidding." The reason why we are offended at God is because we do not like the *Lord* part; it is the lordship that catches us in the throat, because none of us likes to be told what to do. Believing unto salvation is more than giving God a little honorific acknowledgment; it means the once-and-for-all surrender of an independent life to the totality of God's authority.

The messenger must himself be a son or daughter of the resurrection, or he would not be a true witness. The fellowship out of which he comes must be a fellowship where Jesus is Lord in fact, whose members live essentially in the power and reality of resurrection, or there can be no true sending. The whole issue is the truth of resurrection as it is experientially known by a people in the earth, or both unsaved Jew and Gentile will remain bound in their unbelief and self-will. The one who is bringing the good news of a God who reigns is the same one in whom God reigns *in fact*. Though the hearer may not be able to articulate what they are sensing, the truth of His reigning as Lord

---

[11] See Romans 10:9-10

is demonstrated in the posture, the voice, the face, the demeanor and the character of the one who brings the glad tidings.

THE VOICE OF THE PREACHER

There should be the resonance of God in our preaching, not only in the content of the message, but also conveying the disposition of God's own heart, and how *He* feels about what is being said. There is something about the tone of a voice that bespeaks the history and quality of the person's relationship with God. Our voices are as distinctive as our personalities, both of which are tempered by our relationship with God. We look into certain faces and know that they do not reveal the grace of God, nor a relationship with Him of a continuing or deep kind. But there are others who are not even conscious of the radiance emanating from their faces. When you are a seeker after God, and there is a life of communion and devotion, then something of God's essence will be reflected both in your face and your voice. A voice is like a signature. It has been said that by the time we are forty, we are responsible for how our faces look. That would be equally true about our voices. God held Israel responsible for failing to heed both His words and the *voice* of His speaking as it came to them through the prophets.[12]

---

[12] See Jeremiah 7:28

Our Preaching Mandate

Are we secure enough in God that we have nothing to prove? Is our identity established in our union with God? Can we wait for the word that is given without lapsing into human eloquence? If Jesus would not so much as speak His own words, what then shall *we* presume to speak? It is a humbling posture to wait, to be utterly dependent upon God, especially when you are naturally clever in yourself, and have a flair with words.

Even when there is a message to speak, the spirit of the preacher is subject to the preacher. If it is not God's moment to speak, then he is silent. Something happens to him internally when he contains and holds his own spirit until the moment of God's choosing. He knows that every issue is the issue of what glorifies *God*. There is a self-serving dynamic involved when we blurt out something at the wrong moment. We need to come to a place where we have no interest in ourselves; where it is all the same to us whether we speak or not, whether we are seen or not, used or not, set aside or employed. Only *then* can we be used of God.

> I solemnly charge you in the presence of God and of Christ Jesus, who is to judge the living and the dead, and by His appearing and His Kingdom: Preach the word.[13]

A true word is not going to be spoken by those who are ruled by the fear of man.

> Pray on my behalf, that utterance may be

---

[13] 2 Timothy 4:1a-2a

> given to me in the opening of my mouth, to make known with boldness the mystery of the gospel, for which I am an ambassador in chains; that in proclaiming it I may speak boldly, as I ought to speak.[14]

If Paul had to plead for prayer for himself, a man who had an encyclopedic knowledge of apostolic things, then how much more must we set aside any casual approach to the ministry of God's word!

We do not have to bring to the word an additional quality so as to make it more compelling for the hearer. The word speaks for itself. Anyone who would seek to bring an added element through his own personality or manner of speaking is likely bringing a false word. Any exaggeration or sensationalism in the speaking that conjures up a measure of excitement to draw out those who are bored is not true preaching. If we are highly individualistic, and want to cut a swath for ourselves, or do our own thing in our own way, then we are disqualified from giving a true word. God must put His word in our mouth, for His purposes. This is not a surrender of our identity, but an establishing of it *in God*.

COME UP AND BE THERE!

Moses came up into the presence of God that he might receive the tablets of the Law, and right from the very first invitation, we see the whole genius of God with man: "Come up to Me on the mountain and remain there, and I will give you the stone tablets with

---

[14] Ephesians 6:19-20

the law and the commandment which I have written for their instruction."[15] The first requirement of apostolic preaching is ever and always this: "Come up to Me, not for what you are going to receive from Me, but to Me, for My own sake, and *be* there in totality, all that you are in union with all that I am, and *then* I will give you the tablets of the Law."

This is the requirement of God, and it is to this higher ground that He calls the church—the ground of apostolic reality and glory. The whole apostolic message can be summed up in these words: "Come up to Me, and be there." The world is dying for the lack of men and women who can communicate God *as He is in Himself.* The world needs the knowledge of God, exuded by men and women who speak to them out of the presence of God. The world does not know how to live. They have no idea of what it means to be in God's presence. They need to see apostolic reality in those who will teach them how to live, how to *be there* in totality, and how to enjoy the depths of fellowship with both God and their fellow man.

> Such confidence we have through Christ toward God. Not that we are adequate in ourselves to consider anything as coming from ourselves, but our adequacy is from God.[16]

To have a confidence toward God in order to accomplish the works of God cannot be based on our own ability, or anything that is derived from what we are in ourselves. If we are to speak His word, we do not have to buttress it with our own natural personality.

---

[15] Exodus 24:12b
[16] 2 Corinthians 3:4-5

It does not require our charm to make it succeed. The Spirit is given without measure to those who bear His word, and He is quite able and willing to give that word if we will come up to Him and *be* there.

God is looking for candidates who will speak the creative word into the very foundations of the church, words that are given in commandment out of the presence of God by men and women who will come up to Him and be there—up from the fear of men, up from the concern for their own petty reputation. True preaching is not preaching to entertain, but a serious bearing of the word of the Lord. The responsibility is enormous, and we need to know the consequences of it. But when it is spoken, in the moment that it is given of God, it has the potential to bring life to those who live in the shadow of death! The apostolic message, as the proclaimed word, communicates the knowledge and sense of God as He is, thus giving the church its true foundations.

CHAPTER 5

Apostolic Confrontation

Paul on Mars Hill is the sacred man confronting the secular; the spiritual mind pitted against the worldly mind; the heavenly perspective brought into earth and into time. It is an ultimate, classic and eternal confrontation, and therefore every element in this text, and everything that the Spirit of God is expressing through Paul to men, is not only powerfully pertinent in *that* express moment, but continues to reverberate throughout all time and history. It might be said that this episode in Paul's life is more pungent and significant *now* at the conclusion of time and history, than it was two thousand years ago when he spoke it.

> But when the Jews of Thessalonica found out that the word of God had been proclaimed by Paul in Berea also, they came there as well, agitating and stirring up

> the crowds. Then immediately the brethren sent Paul out to go as far as the sea; and Silas and Timothy remained there. Now those who escorted Paul brought him as far as Athens; and receiving a command for Silas and Timothy to come to him as soon as possible, they left.[1]

Paul was fleeing from persecution, and while he was waiting for his colleagues to catch up with him, the Spirit of God set something in motion in his spirit. This is a pure apostolic episode and a revelation of the apostolic man, all the more profound because it was unexpected, unsought, but totally arranged by God.

THE INCEPTION OF PAUL'S MESSAGE

> Now while Paul was waiting for them at Athens, his spirit was being provoked within him as he was observing the city full of idols.[2]

This incident was as much in the intention of God as were all of the other places where Paul found himself. For anyone with an apostolic consciousness, *nothing* is by chance. Everything is ordained by the sovereign hand of God, who attends to every detail. It was all the same to Paul whether he went somewhere because he saw a vision of a Macedonian man calling to him, or whether he went because he was in flight from persecution. If God will not use one means to get his man to the appointed place, then He will use yet

---

[1] Acts 17:13-15
[2] Ibid., v.16

another. We need that same abiding sense of the sovereignty of God, and if we miss a plane, or some untoward thing takes place, we are not to be chafed in our spirits, or murmur under our breath, but rejoice for the inadvertent thing that God will turn to His glory. We should never see ourselves as victims of circumstances, especially when they might seem unpleasant to us. It was not enjoyable for Paul to be in flight from persecution, and yet it is the very thing that God employed to bring His apostolic man to the right place at the right time. Paul never lifted a finger in his own behalf, or in the promotion of his own ministry.

Paul's spirit was grieved and provoked within him as he saw the city wholly given to idolatry. This is the point of inception of any apostolic event. Paul is a man who sees and who grieves, "Now while Paul was waiting ... he was observing." This is a man with his eyes open. He was a true worshipper of God, and that qualified him to discern the things that are false. He was not some hyper-spiritual type that kept himself aloof from the rest of mankind. He saw through the pretensions of men. He knew the world and how it thinks, and he confronted it in the power of God by words that the Lord gave in the moment.

How many of us are grieved in our spirits when we visit the modern-day equivalents of Athens? The Spirit has not ceased grieving; it is that we do not have Paul's proximity to the Spirit. Our eyes are not beholding as God beholds, and therefore we miss the opportunity. The pattern of *every* apostolic and authentic act begins with the stirring of the Spirit in a soul that can be grieved at what he beholds with his eyes.

The Essence of Idolatry

The idolatry that is present with our generation is exactly the same as the idolatry of Paul's day. Idolatry is more than worshipping at pagan altars and shrines. There is an idolatrous spirit that permeates our age. It has been with us since the fall of man. Paul was in Athens, the center of humanism and everything that the world continues to celebrate. Much of present-day philosophy has a direct linkage to the philosophies of that day. Nothing has changed. Epicureanism and Stoicism may not be words commonly used, but the substance of their beliefs still exists today, namely, human philosophies promoted as alternatives to true relationship with God. Athens had a place of prominence in the civilization and glory that was Greece. Athens was known for its love of worldly wisdom, a wisdom that does not make place for the true God.

> So he was reasoning in the synagogue with the Jews and the God-fearing Gentiles, and in the market place every day with those who happened to be present.[3]

Having just witnessed a city given over to idolatry, Paul immediately went and reasoned with the Jews in the synagogue. The synagogue is the place where idolatry is *most rampant* with idolatrous substitution for the true worship of God. We might just as well add the synagogues of the Gentiles, or any religious establishment that offers a religion of

---
[3] Ibid., v.17

convenience, requiring nothing in terms of true union with God.

Idolatry is any religious substitute for the truth of God, the reality of God and the requirement of God. Idols do not require anything from their worshippers, but the Living God insists: "If anyone wishes to come after Me, he must deny himself, and take up his cross and follow Me."[4] An idol is dumb, satisfying the religious needs of men. It is idolatry by whatever name it is called, wherever it is practiced: in the marketplace, the synagogue, or the church.

The apostolic heart continually pounds with a jealousy for the glory of God. It cannot stand to see something that competes for the attention of men, calling itself worship, but is not. If Paul had not been grieved or provoked in his spirit, there would not have been the event that followed. Paul knew that those who are seduced by an idolatrous substitute are doomed eternally. He knew the terror and fear of God, and when God finds such a man, you can be sure that he will be brought to a place of confrontation.

ULTIMATE CONFRONTATION

> And also some of the Epicurean and Stoic philosophers were conversing with him. Some were saying, "What would this idle babbler wish to say?" Others, "He seems to be a proclaimer of strange deities,"— because he was preaching Jesus and the resurrection. And they took him and

---
[4] Matthew 16:24b

> brought him to the Areopagus, saying, "May we know what this new teaching is which you are proclaiming? For you are bringing some strange things to our ears; so we want to know what these things mean." (Now all the Athenians and the strangers visiting there used to spend their time in nothing other than telling or hearing something new.)[5]

Men have never ceased in their quest to understand life and human existence. For the most part, it is a posture that celebrates and exalts man. They *presume* to be seekers after truth, but they never come to the knowledge of the truth. They are always in the process of seeking, but it is with a self-satisfying posture that wants to hear some new thing. Do we see the desolate condition of mankind, the misspent hours, the way it seeks to perpetuate its life? Are our hearts grieved at its condition?

Paul was an itinerant, Hebrew preacher, without any credentials that Greek philosophers could respect or understand. They called him a "babbler" and looked upon him with contempt. He was the antithesis of all that was respected and celebrated by Greek civilization. And yet they were curious, and gave him an opportunity to speak. Paul could not have asked for a more supreme opportunity to bring the message of God to men who represented the highest echelons of a civilization that celebrated itself above God. Therefore, whatever Paul was going to say would be eternally significant.

---

[5] Ibid., vv.18-21

To hear from a true apostle is to be held *eternally* accountable. In what was represented before them, those Athenians came as close to God as is possible on the earth, because it was the High Priest and Apostle of our confession who was being expressed *through* Paul. God cannot do more for men than to put before them the apostolic testimony.

What does a man say when he has to stand before pagans, whose philosophy, mindset and whole civilization are a direct offense against God? What one thing could he say to them for which they would be eternally responsible? That is what the message of Paul on Mars Hill is. His message did not result in a revival; nor is there mention of a new church being established. There were only two or three people who are mentioned by name, who joined themselves to Paul and believed. Why, then, does this episode find a prominent place in the New Testament? Being the capital city of Greece, Athens was the perfect setting for God to confront all that the world looked upon as prestigious, celebrated and wise.

Paul was facing everything that opposed the wisdom of God. Those men whom he faced represented the kingdom of darkness. They may have been clothed with philosophical garb; they may have spoken another kind of language that did not seem too alarming, yet they were as opposed to the kingdom of God as any evil sorcerer. Paul met something head-on, a certain spirit that continues to prevail in the world today. When God confronts it, He confronts it apostolically, which is to say, *foolishly*!

> So Paul stood in the midst of the Areopagus and said, "Men of Athens, I observe that

you are very religious [superstitious][6] in all respects."[7]

If you want to get an intellectual philosopher mad, tell him that he is superstitious. What an indignity! They pride themselves in being *above* superstition, and so, by beginning with an insult, Paul is *already* needling them. He spoke what God gave him to speak without any personal concern for the consequences of that speaking. *This* is the apostolic man. If we are fearful, and walking and speaking in a guarded way, and calculating what we shall say so as not to offend, or be misunderstood, then how shall we be a mouth for God in confrontation with a hostile world? There is only One who can determine what is appropriate in any given moment; namely, the Lord Himself.

> For while I was passing through and examining the objects of your worship, I also found an altar with this inscription, "TO AN UNKNOWN GOD." Therefore what you worship in ignorance, this I proclaim to you."[8]

We will never be able to identify, or confront the thing that is false, unless we can also say with Paul, "this I proclaim to you." It is not enough to know *about* the truth; we need to be intensely and intimately *in* the life of that truth before we dare expose the lie. Paul's statement may sound arrogant, but it is his very boldness and incisiveness that demonstrates the God whom Paul was proclaiming.

Paul mocked them with their superstitious, play-

---

[6] King James Version of the Bible
[7] Ibid., v.22
[8] Ibid., v.23

acting charade about the "Unknown God," as if somehow it shows a respect and reverence, when really it was a phony deceit. Those Athenians may have worshipped their idols ignorantly, but it was a *willful* ignorance. They *chose* to worship a god who is unknown, because an unknown god makes no requirement. It was a phony deference that saves men from any excruciating demand of being in relationship with the God who is. They *prefer* that He remains unknown, but Paul will not allow them that falsity. To come to the true knowledge of God is to have a serious intrusion into your life that changes *everything*.

There is something in the human heart that likes to keep God at a *great* distance. The human heart *wants* an impersonal God, because an impersonal God does not say: "You shall not commit adultery. You shall love the Lord your God with all your heart." Paul's love for his audience was too great to flatter or be ingratiating toward them. He did not spare them, because he knew that truth is painful before it is glorious. True comfort comes after we have been discomforted.

GOD AS CREATOR AND LORD

> The God who made the world and all things in it, since He is Lord of heaven and earth, does not dwell in temples made with hands."[9]

Everything rests upon God as Creator. The earth is the *Lord's*, and therefore He has a right over His

---
[9] Ibid., v.24

own creation. He is not just the Creator of heaven and earth, He is the *Lord* of heaven and earth. But if we do not have a perception of God as Creator, we have no foundation for truth or reality. For Paul, to begin here with God as Creator was not an accident, but a divine revelation of the foundational premise upon which everything rests: "In the beginning God created."

Since He is Lord of heaven and earth, what then is the implication for the city of Athens? He is the *Lord* also of Athens. Paul did not say it in so many words, but it is implicit in what he is saying. Paul could say it with conviction because the Creator of Paul was also his Lord. When Paul used the word "Lord," it would have resonated with certainty. Paul was directly and totally under the authority of the One whom he called Lord, and the evidence was in his very speaking. If the Lord were not Lord, Paul would not have begun with an insult; he would have begun with a compliment the way most of us would, because our speaking is, for the most part, what *we* determine, not what *He* determines.

GOD THE GIVER

> Nor is He served by human hands, as though He needed anything, since He Himself gives to all people life and breath and all things."[10]

Paul was standing in the midst of their pagan temples, more impressive *then* when they stood in their original, pristine beauty. There is something about the visible evidence of this world that is intimidating, but

---

[10] Ibid., v.25

Paul represented another reality, and could say that there was a God who did not need things that men make with their hands, like their monuments, as if He needed anything.

Paul had a knowledge of the God who gives *all* things, including his imprisonment with Silas in Philippi, where they were stripped and beaten to within an inch of their lives. It was an absolutely forsaken place, miles from their friends, yet they were there in obedience to God. At about midnight, the darkest hour, when you give up all hope and confidence, Paul and Silas were praying and singing praises unto God.

Times of adversity and affliction are among the "all things" that come from the hand of God. Can we rejoice in them, and praise God in them, and say with conviction to the unbelievers of this world, that He is the God who gives *all* things? That is what makes an apostle's word so penetrating. He has experienced the "all things," and received them as coming from God's hand. We can *say* that there is a God who gives all things, but it will not mean anything, or have penetration, or be a challenging and compelling statement that demands the attention of men except that it has been tempered into our experience.

If Paul had seen the circumstance of his Philippian imprisonment as a fluke occurrence, he would not have found himself on Mars Hill speaking to Greek philosophers. God is waiting for men who believe that there is a God who gives *all* things. Have we really surrendered to the total sovereignty of God? The evidence is in the way we express our disappointments. We see men as being the problem, or circumstances, or ourselves at fault: "If only *we* had done this instead of that, then something might have been changed." It is not a complete recognition of a supreme God who gives all things. This is not an excuse for our indifference, or neglect, but we need to recognize that He is the God of all things. When we can rejoice in the sovereignty of God when things are painful as well as when things are pleasant, then we can stand before secular men and speak of the God who gives life and breath to all.

THE NATIONS IN PAUL'S MESSAGE

> And He made from one man every nation of mankind to live on all the face of the earth, having determined their appointed times and the boundaries of their habitation.[11]

Rather than the nations being geological accidents, Paul made it clear that they are God's creation, that He has established them, and that He has given them their boundaries. It implies that we are not to make our own boundaries. Wars arise over disputes about territories and land. Mankind does not want to be bound, because a boundary is a limitation, and man does not want to know a God who imposes and requires it.

Paul's view was that God created nations for *His* purposes. Being a purposeful God, He has an intention for the nations, for which reason He established their boundaries and appointed times for their existence. Nations are not accidental entities, or something to be explained by anthropologists. God has established the

---

[11] Ibid., v.26

bounds of the nations. This is contrary to the freethinking of modern men; it is too restrictive for them, and gives them no latitude to use this planet as if it was a playground for *their* own purposes.

THE PURPOSE OF MAN'S EXISTENCE

> That they would seek God, if perhaps they might grope for Him and find Him, though He is not far from each one of us; for in Him we live and move and exist, as even some of your own poets have said, "For we also are His children." Being then the children of God, we ought not to think that the Divine Nature is like gold or silver or stone, an image formed by the art and thought of man.[12]

Without any reference to the scriptures, Paul let them know that the whole purpose of God creating the complex, manifold civilizations, the nations and races, was so that the nations might seek God, if perhaps they might grope for Him and find Him. The history of the world, its economies, its technologies, its architecture and its institutions, are only secondary things to provide sufficient stability and order for life, so that men might seek God.

Paul reduced the whole purpose of human life on this planet to one pursuit only; namely, to seek and find God *before* we enter into eternity. The purpose of man's existence is not to seek his happiness, but to seek God. To find happiness outside of God is a

---

[12] Ibid., vv.27-29

delusion and deception. God is the Creator and the Lord of heaven and earth, but He has not established nations for us to pursue our careers, promote our interests and build our civilizations.

The message that we can live and move and exist *in* God is unwelcome to the ears of mankind. They do not *want* to know of such a possibility. They do not *want* to be bound by their habitations; they do not *want* to come under the purposes of God. Every single syllable that came from Paul's lips is a calculated offense to the sensibilities and mindset of man. They do not want to be restricted, and therefore they prefer to have their monuments to the "Unknown God." Paul declared the nature of God, the purpose of God and the requirement of God. It is a declaration that men do not want to hear. It is not only contrary to their opinions, it altogether contradicts the whole foundation and structure of their thought and value systems.

THE PURPOSE OF NATIONS

"That they would seek God." For a long time I thought that the "they" referred exclusively to individuals, and in a sense that is true, but it would be more exegetically correct to see the "they" as referring to the *nations* whose boundaries, habitations and times were established by God. Paul is implying that the *nations* should seek God for the reason for which they were established. The failure to consult God is the evidence that mankind prefers self-will and self-determination. It is for this reason that God calls every man to repent, because He has chosen a day in which He will judge the *nations* for their scandalous rejection of Him. The great love that the church can demonstrate to their nations is to save them from the judgment of God by saying: "God has a controversy with you."

The nations do not seek God, because they do not *want* to be found. Who wants to find Him if the revelation that comes with that discovery is injurious or threatening to their own self-interest? Their conduct and indifference speak for themselves. Their ignorance is willful, and their failure to seek God for His purpose has been unbelievably tragic for mankind. Wars, conflicts, devastations and death have been the result of self-seeking, autonomous nations acting out of their ambition and rivalry for glory and fame.

The nations need to be told, which is not to say that they will listen, but if we know that judgment is coming, and we do not sound a warning, then their blood is on our hands. It is unlikely that governments will respond, but individuals hearing the message and seeing our colossal faith and insistence upon it, will be stung in their hearts. Those who have treated the issue of God with a casual attitude will now be alerted to something that might be salvational for them.

To find God is to find Him for the purpose for which we were created. There is no finding of God, nor is there any knowledge of God that is a true knowledge, independent of His revealed purpose. He is a purposeful God by very definition, or else He would not be God. To think that we have found God, and yet *not* to have found Him for His purpose, is *not* to have found God. You may have a measure of enjoyment and fulfillment, but the true discovery of God is the knowledge of God as the God who has purpose. And it is in the seeking of Him for that purpose that we come into the truth and depth of *true* union with God. Yet, to only seek Him for the sense of His presence, which is characteristic of contemporary church life, and not to seek Him for His purpose, is not to seek Him as He desires to be sought. The true believer will seek God to find out and know the purpose for His creation. The same principle applies to nations.

THE NATIONS IN RELATION TO ISRAEL

God Himself has established the boundaries of the nations, and yet there is something about the nature of nationhood that encourages patriotism, which is an idolatrous preoccupation with one's nation. Men will die for their nations. God made a provision to keep nations in certain boundaries and in relationships that would be sane and healthy for them, and yet allow Him to be the recognized Head over all. There is a legitimate place for nations, but only within a certain structure that God Himself has provided.

> When the Most High gave the nations their inheritance, when He separated the sons of man, He set the boundaries of the peoples according to the number of the sons of Israel.[13]

God has made *Israel* central to all the nations, and nations cannot be related to God, or come under the purposes of God, independent of their submission to the centrality of Israel. In other words, there will never

---

[13] Deuteronomy 32:8

be peace and justice in the world until the nations come back to God's original intention for them.

> Thus says the Lord God, "This is Jerusalem; I have set her at the center of the nations, with lands around her."[14]

This is not just the issue of God's strategy and design; it is the issue of God *as God*. That is why men oppose it. By appointing what He appoints and choosing what He chooses, God makes known the way in which He wants *Himself* to be understood. In other words, it is more than the issue of real estate. Nations want to be autonomous; they want to choose their own future, perform their own will, and seek their *own* glory. However, the very existence of Israel in the world is a stubborn reminder for the nations that there is a God to whom they do not wish to surrender their self-will.

Therefore, to remove Israel is to remove God's righteous demand upon the nations. That is one of the reasons why Jews have been the object of near annihilation throughout their history—though their own sinful conduct has justified the wrath of God being poured out upon them. Both things are true at the same time. Nations have been ventilating their hatred against God for millennia by seeking to destroy the Jew, but the destruction that has been visited upon the Jew is a deserved judgment, in exact proportion to their sinful rejection of God. The greatest drama of the last days is the attempt by the nations to annihilate Israel so as to remove God's very provision for their

---

[14] Ezekiel 5:5

relatedness to Him.[15]

THE HEART OF PAUL'S MESSAGE

> Therefore having overlooked the times of ignorance, God is now declaring to men that all people everywhere should repent, because He has fixed a day in which He will judge the world in righteousness through a Man whom He has appointed, having furnished proof to all men by raising Him from the dead.[16]

In that one statement, Paul sums up the apostolic message: Judgment—Resurrection—A Man—A Day. Paul was utterly specific and absolute, and mankind does not like to be boxed in with something that is so explicit and demanding because it means that they can no longer construct gods of their own imagining. For Paul, anything less than this message would have been doing a disservice to his hearers. That God *will* judge *all* men is chilling in its totality. Whatever justification there might have been for your ignorance before, there is no longer any excuse, because there is now a people in the earth who not only proclaim, but also demonstrate the reality of His resurrection.

God is patient, but there is a day coming when His wrath will be expressed. It is called the "day of the Lord," and it will come against the nations of the world *after* He has dealt with Israel. He begins with the house of God, but no nation will be exempt from the

---

[15] See Author's book: *The Mystery of Israel and the Church*
[16] Acts 17:30-31

fury of God poured out in wrath against them. That is why Paul is warning them in Athens. Jesus is not just King of the Jews; He is God's theocratic ruler over His *entire* creation, including all the nations.

There is nothing more foolish than to bear the message of judgment, especially in a world that is doing what is right in its own sight. We can measure how deep we really are in God, and how much our own hearts have been affected by the truth of a day of judgment, by our willingness to express it to another. The "day of the Lord" is at the door. We know it technically, but do we know it actually? Can we say it to Epicureans and Stoics with conviction? Paul knew God as Judge, and could therefore speak of judgment with conviction.

If the message two thousand years ago was a call to repentance, what shall *we* say who are living that much closer to the day of judgment? Do we have the same sense of urgency that Paul knew? The early church was not deceived into thinking that the Judge was at the door; the issue is not chronological, but expectation and urgency. This dynamic of expectation is intrinsic to any true apostolic church. Do we see this expectation as being the logic of our faith? Do we bring it to bear on all of our decisions? Are we planning ahead for next year's vacation? By our actual conduct, we betray what we purport to believe. Does our very presence compel men to a place of repentance? Does our speaking to men guarantee that they will be without excuse on the day of judgment?

The Nations in the Light of Judgment

The nations are in rebellion against God. The increasing number of nations over the centuries is only one statement of it; their false gods are another, while their opposition to Israel is the most graphic expression of their rebellion. The millennial peace paves the way for the nations to come into God's ordained configuration. Israel is at the center; the Law goes forth out of Zion. The nations come up to Jerusalem at the Feast of Tabernacles to pay respect to the God of Israel. That is how God intended it from the first, but He has first to deal with the rebellion in His own nation, whom He has chosen, and then with the nations who are also in rebellion against Him.

This is the apostolic setting that the church needs to be inducted into. Without it, we condemn ourselves to goals and purposes that center in ourselves, our success and our perpetuation.

> "For behold, I am beginning to work calamity in this city which is called by My name, and shall you be completely free from punishment? You will not be free from punishment; for I am summoning a sword against all the inhabitants of the earth," declares the LORD of hosts. "Therefore you shall prophesy against them all these words, and you shall say to them, 'The LORD will roar from on high and utter His voice from His holy habitation; He will roar mightily against His fold. He will shout like those who tread the grapes, against all the inhabitants of the earth. A

> clamor has come to the end of the earth, because the LORD has a controversy with the nations. He is entering into judgment with all flesh; as for the wicked, He has given them to the sword,' declares the LORD."[17]

The day of the Lord, so central to the apostolic and prophetic mindset, will be the great day when the wrath of God will be released in fury against the nations. It will be a time of unspeakable devastation. But God will not bring His judgment until the nations have heard warnings. The church has not yet performed this to any significant degree. We have ourselves been caught up at the individual level, and therefore have not considered God's message to the nations. I am expecting that there will be an apostolic entity in the earth, bearing the authority and message of Paul to the nations, before the judgment promised by God falls. For many of us, the day of the Lord has no cogent meaning. We know it exists; it has a familiar ring, but it is not yet central to our own consideration and understanding.

> And with many other words he [Peter] solemnly testified and kept on exhorting them, saying, "Be saved from this perverse generation!"[18]

Peter was addressing those who had come up to Jerusalem for the high feast days. His appeal to them was to be saved out of the judgment coming upon the nation. He preached the day of the Lord as being at hand, the evidence being the signs, the wonders in the

---

[17] Jeremiah 25:29-31
[18] Acts 2:40

sky, blood and fire, the sun being turned into darkness, and the speaking in other tongues, all of which were foretold by the prophet Joel. "Be saved" did not mean salvation as we commonly understand it today. It was a salvation out of the judgment that is coming with wrath upon the nations. *This* is the apostolic message of the last days. As it was at the first, so shall it be at the end. Our present gospel has made salvation something much less and other than what God intended, and we have therefore missed the larger context of God's wrath that is to be exhibited toward the nations in the day of the Lord.

Mankind has no sense of an end to this present age, no sense of an imminent judgment. Nevertheless, this message needs to be communicated *before* the coming judgment. To be able to convey that reality means that there has to be an imminent sense of God as Judge by those who have first opened themselves to some expression of that reality in their own lives. To omit God in His judgment is to dismiss God as He desires to be known.

Do we really have a message for individuals if we have not a message for the nation? If we cannot confront the corporate sin, can we really confront the individual sin? The failure to identify sin as sin has made our evangelism shallow, based on the benefit one receives in acknowledging the atoning work of God on the cross.

We have not really had an effectual gospel to individuals because we have not shown them their sin in the context of the sins of their nations. The sins of the nations are the same as the individuals who comprise the nations. Far from the message of the gospel to the nations being seen as an alternative to the gospel to individuals, it may well be *the key* to bringing the gospel to individuals. Men have a difficulty in seeing *their* sin as sin. That is the nature of sin; it disguises itself as not being sin, and is rationalized away. But the conduct of nations as nations is so blatant and conspicuous that it cannot help but be seen.

RESURRECTION—THE POWER OF PAUL'S MESSAGE

We have got to be to the nations what Paul was to Athens. Paul could say that God has appointed a day in which He will judge the world, "having furnished proof to all men by raising Him [Jesus] from the dead."[19] The validity of Paul's message rested entirely on the resurrection of Jesus from the dead. His audience was eternally accountable on the basis of an event for which they most likely had no awareness. How could Paul expect them to believe the resurrection when the Jewish nation themselves rejected it? His hearers likely had no biblical framework, and yet Paul holds them accountable, and puts them under every obligation to understand it *unto repentance*.

For Paul, the issue of the resurrection of Jesus was not just a viewpoint only to be expressed on Sundays in a religious environment, but totally relevant in the affairs of men in the world *now*. There is nothing more pertinent for secular men than the subject of God, and the truths of God, despite the offense it will bring

---
[19] Acts 17:31b

to the hearers. The apostolic mindset, which is the definitive mind of God, brings the divine view, whether it is accepted or not.

Everything that came out of Paul was incarnate *in* him. Paul did not just proclaim the message of the gospel; he *was* the visible demonstration of it; he was the word made flesh. Those Athenians heard a convicting word, coming out of the mouth of a man who was steeped in the reality of what he was proclaiming. That is what made him an apostle, and those who reject *that* witness are rejecting the finest of what God can present to men. There is nothing more that God can do in His mercy. Then shall the end come. Their only basis for believing in the phenomenon of resurrection was that Paul was himself *in* the resurrection. He was a man raised up out of death. His speech to the Athenians was itself a resurrection phenomenon. It was God's very own statement given in God's very own power.

> Now when they heard of the resurrection of the dead, some began to sneer, but others said, "We shall hear you again concerning this." So Paul went out of their midst. But some men joined him and believed, among whom also were Dionysius the Areopagite and a woman named Damaris and others with them.[20]

Those who believed the message joined themselves *to Paul*, and believed. Paul *was* the message, rather than an abstract conveyor of a technical word of truth. There was something about

---

[20] Acts 17:32-34

the reality of his life, something that exuded from his own spirit, which, in itself, was the resurrection. He was already a man in eternity, a citizen of heaven, and living already in the power of the age to come. It was a statement of his apostolic life, and it needs to be a statement of ours also.

The reality and the power of the resurrection had to be demonstrated there on Mars Hill to the Greeks. If the resurrection life was not demonstrated through Paul himself, then it would only have been an abstract concept. Paul said that God had given proof to all men, because the very life and speaking that came out of Paul were the demonstration of a resurrected and ascended King, whose kingship, love, and conviction were pouring out of that beggarly Hebrew vessel.

When Jesus appeared to His disciples in His resurrection body, we read that they did not believe "unto joy." There is something so profoundly deep in our human nature that opposes the supernatural, that even when it is demonstrated in the person of Jesus Himself, there is unbelief. He ate before them in His resurrection body, yet their carnal minds were so opposed to the supernatural God that they staggered over the issue of the resurrection.

True faith is when we are *living* in the power of the life we say we believe in. Is our life hidden with Christ in God? When *His* life is revealed, our life shall be revealed also with Him *unto glory*. For many years, I could not understand why there was such a painful absence of the glory of God upon the earth and in God's people. There are many correct believers, living good, moral lives and who are models of propriety, but where is the glory? The glory is only in the resurrection life and power that comes when we are dead and hidden with Christ in God. There are so few believers who have attained to *this* faith, to *this* resurrection, to *this* reality and to *this* supernatural basis, which may be the very reason why we do not proclaim it to men.

THE FINALITY OF PAUL'S MESSAGE

Paul lived in eternity, and therefore brought an urgency to every situation he encountered. Those Athenians will be without excuse. They were confronted with the visible foretaste of the age to come. The gospel was preached to them with authority and power, compelling them to decide *for* or *against* God.

What are *our* foundations if they are not the same as Paul's? Can we, with him, see what is invisible as being more impressive than what is temporal and visible? Athens was a mighty city, one of the great glories of the ancient world, yet Paul walked right through it wholly unimpressed. It was the world, which was soon to pass away. In a moment of time, Paul's audience heard a man who had no qualifications or credentials from their intellectual point of view. They shall be held eternally responsible for how they responded to that heaven-sent messenger proclaiming the soon-coming day of judgment. Can we say the same of those to whom we presently speak?

CHAPTER 6

Apostolic Character

Meekness is that quality of character by which we shall be able to discern those who "call themselves apostles, and they are not."[1] Presumptuous apostles are going to be one of the dangers of the last days. They will seem to have a measure of authority and knowledge that will impress the undiscerning. However, there is one measure of authenticity that cannot be feigned or emulated; namely, *true* meekness. We cannot go to a school to learn to be meek. Meekness is something attained by those who are in union with God, who is Himself meek, humble and lowly of heart.

Moses, who wrote the first five books of the Bible, could say of himself: "Now the man Moses was very humble, more than any man who was on the face of the

---

[1] See Revelation 2:2

earth."[2] It sounds like arrogance of spirit, but when a man can speak that of himself, knowing he cannot take to himself any acknowledgment for that condition, then he has an ultimate humility. It was God's grace that had brought him to that meekness. Humility is not something that man can develop as a character trait independent of God. Humility is what God is in Himself, and the only one who can exhibit humility is that one who has been consistently in the presence of God's humility. It is humbling to be there, and that is why Moses could make that statement, not as a credit to himself, but to God, out of whose presence that humility was established.

When Moses came down from the mount with the tablets of the Law, he saw Israelites dancing around the golden calf they had fashioned. Burning with indignation, he threw down and broke the tablets that God had written on with His finger. He then commanded that the golden calf be ground to powder, and told the people to drink it. He made them drink their idol, and there is not a single complaint or whimper of opposition to that requirement. His authority was such that no one took issue with that requirement.

Then Moses asked who was going to be on the Lord's side. The Levites came forward, and they were told to put their swords on their side, go into the camp, and slay all those who had worshipped at the false idol. What authority for the man who was the meekest in all the earth! There is a conjunction between humility and authority. Only the meek have authority in God. Moses' meekness was the statement of his union with

---

[2] Numbers 12:3

God by which God's very own character was imparted to him.

The apostle Paul himself was unsparing in telling things the way they needed to be spoken. He rebuked, exhorted, beseeched and pleaded. But he did not flaunt his apostolic credentials, nor did he employ his authority to coerce and manipulate. How we use our authority reveals what we are, and someone has said that what we do with the weakest and the least in our midst reveals the truth of our heart condition before God. So when a government begins to oppress and persecute the weak and defenseless, it is revealing its true, ugly character.

HUMILITY AND OBEDIENCE

The issue of humility is paradoxical, because the apostle is so single-eyed, adamant and utterly persuaded about the rightness of his word; but others will construe that posture as seeming arrogance. The false apostle will *appear* humble, something like a salesman's "humility" that is exaggerated in order to sell the product. He wants the favor and approval of men, to be seen as a nice guy, and therefore, he will always seem to be reasonable, quiet and diplomatic. He puts something above and before God; namely, his own self-consideration.

The Lord Himself was absolute, and used words in a fierce way. When we think of meekness, we think of mild, quiet and deferring. But if we see meekness as total obedience to God, all the more in an act or a word that gives an impression to the contrary, then we will have a greater understanding of its reality. The obedient servant, one whose total passion is for the glory of God, may even receive reproach for being too zealous. True humility is reflected in true obedience.

An apostle will not relent or refrain when God requires him to speak. He shuns the distinctions and honors that men accord each other. He necessarily has to, or there would be a compromise of what he is in God. He is naturally unaffected, normal and unprepossessing in appearance and demeanor, despising what is showy, sensational or bizarre. A false apostle can be identified as one who gives the impression of being self-confident and self-assured, always in his dignity, or he carries himself in a way that encourages you to notice his calling.

"The true character of the loveliness that tells for God is always unconscious [unaware of itself]," wrote Oswald Chambers. True spirituality is unself-conscious; it is *mindless* about itself. It is the very quality exhibited by Jesus; although He knew who He was, and disputed with the doctors of the Law at the age of twelve, His whole earthly ministry had a remarkable quality of unselfconsciousness about it. He was not a man who went around telling what ministry He was called to.

The Broken Alabaster Vial

There is an episode in the life of Jesus, hardly worth mentioning you would think, and yet God includes it in three of the gospels in one form or another:

> While He was in Bethany at the home of

> Simon the leper, and reclining at the table, there came a woman with an alabaster vial of very costly perfume of pure nard; and she broke the vial and poured it over His head. But some were indignantly remarking to one another, "Why has this perfume been wasted? For this perfume might have been sold for over three hundred denarii, and the money given to the poor." And they were scolding her.
>
> But Jesus said, "Let her alone; why do you bother her? She has done a good deed to Me. For you always have the poor with you, and whenever you wish you can do good to them; but you do not always have Me. She has done what she could; she has anointed My body beforehand for the burial. Truly I say to you, wherever the gospel is preached in the whole world, what this woman has done will also be spoken of in memory of her."
>
> Then Judas Iscariot, who was one of the twelve, went off to the chief priests in order to betray Him to them. They were glad when they heard this, and promised to give him money. And he began seeking how to betray Him at an opportune time.[3]

The disciples of Jesus considered what she had done as being a waste. Efficiency and utility are the spirit of our age. We will only do something if we get something in return. But something that is given

---
[3] Mark 14:3-11

lavishly, without any thought of return, is a costly act of self-sacrifice. The disciples recoiled in indignation, and murmured against this woman: "For what purpose was this waste. That expensive ointment could have been sold, and the proceeds used to buy tracts, finance ministries and all those wonderfully helpful things."

The woman came bearing an exquisite alabaster vial. Remarkably, the only way to extract the ointment was to break the container. There was no screw-off cap that could be neatly screwed back on for the next time. She either had to break it in order to extract the contents, or the contents would remain enclosed. That is a beautiful picture of ourselves, shaped at the hand of God, vials of expensive material, but however outwardly impressive we are in that sense, it will *not* make us significant to a dying world, and especially to the Jewish people. Any true significance we might have for God is related to the fragrance of the knowledge of Him made manifest by us in every place.

We all emit a particular fragrance. With some, the aroma is exquisite, but with others it is rather ordinary. It depends very much upon what kind of history we have with God. We can have the fragrance of Christ formed in us through identification with Him in His sufferings, or we can have the religion of convenience, which, in the final analysis, is also the religion of betrayal. If our Christianity costs nothing, and is convenient, we are already one with Judas. The faith is extraordinarily demanding, and that is why Jesus commended what the woman had done, and it was to be a memorial to her wherever *this* gospel is preached. The gospel is the gospel of extravagant abandonment and pouring out, or it is not the gospel.

Jesus loved this woman: "She has done a good deed to Me." She came with something very precious and expensive, into a room full of men bristling with indignation, but she did not let that deter her

Watchman Nee has said that the principle of waste is the principle of power. We lack life-changing power because we have not emptied ourselves out before God, and therefore we condemn ourselves to a religion of convenience. We are antiseptic and correct, but we are not fragrant. We are not lavish with each other, afraid to take the risks of that kind of intensity of relationship by which true formation of character takes place. We satisfy ourselves with a religion of convenience, namely, a Sunday service and midweek Bible study, and then retreat home to our own privacy.

There is something about brokenness in God's sight that is so dear to Him. It was exemplified in His own body at the cross, and He is waiting for the same thing in His church, namely, a broken and contrite people who will exude the fragrance of Christ. Something more than correctness and well-wishing intention are required. The meekness of brokenness comes when we break and pour out, that the fragrance of God might be emitted.

MEEKNESS: THE KEY TO REVELATION

The apostles and prophets are given the stewardship of the mysteries of God. One of the keys to the revelation of the mysteries is found in the book of Ephesians:

> To me, the very least of all saints, this grace was given, to preach to the Gentiles the unfathomable riches of Christ.[4]

All true seeing is given to men who, like Paul, see themselves as the very least of all saints. Paul was not being deferential and polite; this was Paul's actual, heartfelt consciousness of how he saw himself before God. He was the apostle to whom was afforded such lofty visions that God had to give him a thorn in his side, lest he be exalted beyond measure for the magnitude of the revelations that were given him. To see one's self as least is the deepest humility.

Ironically, the deeper we come into the knowledge of God the more we see ourselves as the least of all men. Instead of becoming more exalted by the increase of our knowledge, the further we go down and see how abased and pitiful we really are. It is a seeming contradiction that can be found only in a believer. Meekness is a work of God that comes out of relationship with Him. It is the revelation of God, as He is, that brings a man to see himself as least. The revelation of what we are is altogether related to the revelation of who He is.

> Then I [Isaiah] said, "Woe is me, for I am ruined! Because I am a man of unclean lips, and I live among a people of unclean lips; for my eyes have seen the King, the LORD of hosts."[5]

This is the "prince" of the prophets speaking, a foundational man, who was given a glimpse of God as

---

[4] Ephesians 3:8
[5] Isaiah 6:5

He in fact is. God is not as *we* think Him to be. For many of us, God is a projection of the way we would *like* Him to be, especially when we have chosen to celebrate one attribute of God while ignoring another. The *key* knowledge is the knowledge of God as He is. Foundational men are those who can communicate God in *that* knowledge.

THE TWO WITNESSES

> And I will grant authority to my two witnesses, and they will prophesy for twelve hundred and sixty days, clothed in sackcloth. These are the two olive trees and the two lampstands that stand before the LORD of the earth. And if anyone wants to harm them, fire flows out of their mouth and devours their enemies; so if anyone wants to harm them, he must be killed in this way.
>
> These have the power to shut up the sky, so that rain will not fall during the days of their prophesying; and they have power over the waters to turn them into blood, and to strike the earth with every plague, as often as they desire.[6]

These men will be dressed in sackcloth, clothed in humility, clothed in the meekness of God. Any humility that is obtained through self-conscious determination is necessarily false. The humility of God is a prerequisite for the authority of God, of being

---

[6] Revelation 11:3-6

able to "shut up the sky." God can only commit such remarkable dimensions to those who are in authentic union with Him, the evidence of which is their meekness and humility. The sackcloth is not an external thing, although I am sure it will be worn; it was rather a statement of an inward condition that cannot be copied, that cannot be learned by modulating our voices, or being self-effacing. Either it is, or it is not; and if it is, it will be in proportion to our union with God in the fellowship of His sufferings. This is how we obtain and maintain a condition of humility, essential for the overcoming and authentically spiritual life.

Jesus knew He was the Son of God, sent of the Father, and yet He walked through life with a selflessness and mindlessness about His own calling. Paul could say: "Imitate me as I imitate Christ." Yet, there is no sense of arrogance in his statements.

BLAMELESS CONSISTENCY

> For our gospel did not come to you in word only, but also in power and in the Holy Spirit and with full conviction; just as you know what kind of men we proved to be among you for your sake.[7]

There is a theme struck in this verse that needs to penetrate our deepest consciousness. Our modern life tends to be set in compartments: the secular and the sacred, everyday life and the religious, the private person and the public minister, and yet Paul did not

---

[7] 1 Thessalonians 1:5

know those distinctions. He was one true man through and through, the full-orbed man. The apostle is the thing in himself, the word made flesh, and that is why Paul could continually offer *himself* as an example. He did not say, "Follow my principles!" but, "Follow me!" It is what an apostle is in himself, in Christ, that is the foundation of the church. We are to be one true thing throughout, day in and day out. Paul was instant in season and out, always ready, always appropriate, before Jews and Greeks. God's call is for an entire church to be like that.

The power of the gospel came with full conviction to the Thessalonians in exact proportion to the quality, character and manner of men Paul and his co-laborers proved to be among them. Paul was not ashamed to remind them that the testimony of what *he* proved to be was the key witness by which they were saved. They knew Paul as the same, consistent thing, and this was altogether related to the word that came to them in power. There was no professional ministerial mystique in Paul by which he was something else privately.

There are only two ruling passions in an apostolic man—for your sake and for God's sake. It was never for *my* sake. Paul had no interest in himself, or for himself. These two considerations are the necessary requirements for an apostle, and therefore an apostolic church. The superstructure must be of the same kind as the foundation. In his farewell address to the elders in Ephesus, Paul writes:

> You yourselves know, from the first day that I set foot in Asia, how I was with you the whole time, serving the Lord with all

> humility and with tears and with trials which came upon me through the plots of the Jews.[8]

Regardless of his outward circumstances, there was a precious consistency of character. This is something far beyond good intentions, and there is only one way to explain this kind of consistency, as in Paul's own words: "For to me, to live is Christ." Paul is being quite literal. This is the *only* answer, and we cannot seek to be apostolic, or true, on the basis of human determination by which we bite our lips, not knowing what we ought to be doing. We *will* fail, and we will fail wretchedly. We *must* find the reality that Paul found, and it is just as available to us as it was to him.

In a certain sense, Paul's life was the continuation of the life of the crucified and resurrected Christ, who had found for Himself another vessel wholly yielded to His life. It was a Paul who had no life unto himself, or for himself, and who could say, "I am crucified with Christ, nevertheless I live, yet not I." Is *our* gospel going forth in the power of the Spirit, and in full conviction? In his letter to the Thessalonians, Paul writes:

> For they themselves report about us what kind of a reception we had with you, and how you turned to God from idols to serve a living and true God, and to wait for His Son from heaven, whom He raised from the dead, that is Jesus, who rescues us from the

---

[8] Acts 20:18b-19

wrath to come.[9]

For all of our modern-day, innocuous evangelism and flashy evangelists, can it be said that the proclamation of the gospel is turning pagans from their idols to serve the true and living God? We are content if men will only "accept" Christ and attend Christian services. Our evangelism has become a statistical game whereby we count the number of decisions made. Paul's gospel had another consequence; it turned men from their idols to serve the living God. Our whole standard needs to be elevated again to the apostolic level, for this alone is God's. Like Paul, we need to become wholly abandoned to the purposes of God. Paul writes:

> And now, behold, bound by the Spirit, I am on my way to Jerusalem, not knowing what will happen to me there, except that the Holy Spirit solemnly testifies to me in every city, saying that bonds and afflictions await me. But I do not consider my life of any account as dear to myself.[10]

We see the divine character wrought in a man who was originally a persecutor and a murderer. Paul did not consider his life of any account as dear to himself, and we shall never have the power and authority to turn men from their idols so long as *we* hold our lives as dear to *ourselves*.

> But this I say, brethren, the time has been shortened, so that from now on those who have wives should be as though they had

---
[9] 1 Thessalonians 1:9-10
[10] Acts 20:22-24a

> none; and those who weep, as though they did not weep; and those who rejoice, as though they did not rejoice; and those who buy, as though they did not possess; and those who use the world, as though they did not make full use of it; for the form of this world is passing away. But I want you to be free from concern.[11]

The whole purpose of this apostolic exhortation is that we may attend upon the Lord without distraction, for the time is short! Paul said that almost two thousand years ago, but how many of us believe it now? At the time of his writing, the converts lived in the expectation of a soon-coming, apocalyptic conclusion. Are we anticipating continually the things that shall shortly come to pass? For that very reason, we must be indifferent to the various fads and fashions of our day, which are going to pass away. Have we come to the place where we are not moved by outward and visible things? Yes, we can handle them and use them, but they do not have a power over us. Paul was a heavenly man. He sought to finish his course and the ministry that he had received of the Lord.

> You are witnesses, and so is God, how devoutly and uprightly and blamelessly we behaved toward you believers.[12]

Paul had an acute awareness that before God we are utterly transparent. God sees us in our public moments as well as our private thoughts. He sees us at all times, and our lives must be *consciously* lived in His sight and in that knowledge. This is the only true

---

[11] 1 Corinthians 7:32a
[12] 1 Thessalonians 2:10

motivation for blamelessness, and we shall never be blameless until we have it. The way we so often conduct ourselves privately and personally is a remarkable effrontery toward God. It is really a statement to the fact that we do not believe that our lives are being lived in His sight.

Paul writes about being found blameless at the Lord's coming. He says that others may strive for a corruptible crown, but we for an incorruptible one. For Paul, it was too shameful to consider that he should come before the Lord and not have a crown to lay at His feet. Do we have any desire to win a crown? The crown of glory shall not exceed the crown of our suffering! If we are unwilling for the crown of thorns, the trials, the demands, the reproaches and the sufferings for righteousness' sake in order to learn what it means to live a heavenly life in an inhospitable earth, then we shall not have a crown to lay before Him.

We are not going to obtain blamelessness in a day, but we will not obtain it at all if we do not consciously see it as a reality to be desired. We need to see the necessity of moving from our present fear of men to the restoration of the fear of God. This must be our apostolic goal and mission for which we need the participation of the brethren. We are *all* in this together.

Church must be the one place in the earth where we do not have to put on any appearance, where we can frankly acknowledge our defects and imperfections, and speak to one another the truth in love, exhorting one another *daily*. Next Sunday is already too late. In fact, mere Sundays will never accomplish this. Exhorting one another daily while it is yet today means a radical alteration of our present lifestyle. It calls for the establishing of a whole new set of priorities that will make a serious intrusion upon our privacy and time. It is a necessary review that has the potential to pave the way for true apostolic character and living.

This requires a closely-knit body of believers being to one another what they must, that they might grow up unto Him in all things, who is the Head, even Christ. It is the end of passivity in the church, looking up to the platform while one man more or less conducts the whole service. We need to find and make room to speak face-to-face, rather than looking at the back of each other's heads. We need to be seeing in each other's *faces* the glory of God, and moving from glory to glory. This kind of matrix of living will open our lives up, and place us under review before man and before God.

Conclusion

This is only a gleaning from the vineyard of Paul, just a chance phrase here and there from his epistles, but what a standard begins to emerge! It is the apostolic standard that Paul himself walked in and exhibited. "Follow me, be imitators of me," needs again to be said. It is kingdom living. If you want to know what God is like, then see this humility, see this uncompromising truth, see this integrity, see this righteousness, see this godly character. How many will subscribe to that standard from this day forth?

Apostolic is the Lord in all of the incarnate

fullness occupying the human frame. Can you imagine a church like that, a whole church from top to bottom, in the same apostolic splendor, the same apostolic stature, the same apostolic character, the same apostolic witness and the same apostolic power? That is what God is wanting.

CHAPTER 7

Apostolic Conversion

The apostolic realities that pertain to God's glory can only find fulfillment in a people who are utterly abandoned to God. If we embrace only the vocabulary of apostolicity, we engage the cruelest of all deceptions. It is possible to be saved, and yet not be converted in the sense of an utterness toward God that apostolic reality requires. Something foundational to our relationship with God must first be brought into being, a radical crossing from the one reality to the other.

In the book of Acts, there are three records of Paul's conversion.[1] Paul's apostolic life following that conversion was altogether proportionate to the kind of beginning that it had. Many of us need that same beginning, which, if it is not made, will condemn us to

---

[1] Acts 9:1-16; Acts 22:5-11; Acts 26:10-18

a certain stagnant level of Christian life, beneath what the Lord intensely desires.

There is a parallel between where God's people stand today and where Israel stood on the banks of the Jordan, being required to make that great crossing over with Joshua and Caleb. Jordan means "a descent into death," and there is surely a Jordan before most of us. The Israelites had stumbled about in the religious wasteland for forty years. With the exception of Caleb and Joshua, an entire generation died in the desert because they did not have a heart to participate in the taking of the land of promise. We stand at this kind of crossroad today; it is time to cross over.

Not every tribe of Israel crossed over. Manasseh, Reuben and a portion of Gad chose to remain where they were because the ground was fertile and the grasses high. They were cattle breeders who focused solely on things of *immediate* value. They were unwilling for the risk of what might be found on the other side. They pleaded with Moses, got what they wanted, and have been subsequently lost to the history of Israel.

The Gadarenes are mentioned in the New Testament, a melancholy reminder of the tribe of Gad. They raised pigs, and were unwilling to receive the Messiah of Israel, preferring to sustain their herds, rather than welcome Him who cast those same herds into the sea! The unwillingness to cross over has tragic consequences. The reason is always the same—it is not conducive to the "flesh." We prefer the assurance of things that pertain to "herds," to our immediate self-interest and gratification.

> Now Saul, still breathing threats and murder against the disciples of the Lord, went to the high priest, and asked for letters from him to the synagogues at Damascus, so that if he found any belonging to the Way, both men and women, he might bring them bound to Jerusalem.
>
> As he was traveling, it happened that he was approaching Damascus, and suddenly a light from heaven flashed around him; and he fell to the ground and heard a voice saying to him, "Saul, Saul, why are you persecuting Me?"[2]

Saul's conversion was a "crossing over." It begins with the phrase: "As he was traveling." There is more hope for an enemy of God journeying in full sincerity, even in his error, than for those who purport to be the friends of God, who have long since ceased journeying, who are just treading water, and occupying a much safer place. There is more hope to convert an enemy in motion, however grievous his error, than there is for those of us who are safely installed in correct doctrines, but who are not moving forward at all. Would there have been a conversion if Saul had been satisfied with the conventional categories of religious orthodoxy and the spiritual *status quo* of his life? But as he was traveling, *suddenly* there came a light from heaven. When the Lord saw that questing, a willingness to be traveling on the way, He sent His light from heaven.

---

[2] Acts 9:1-4

Saul fell to the ground, and heard a voice saying to him: "Saul, Saul, why are *you* persecuting *Me*?" Our every error is putting our "you" before, over and above, God's "Me." In other words, "why do you put *your* self-interest, however religious and sanctified you think it to be, *before* Me?" We are not truly converted until God's "Me" is *before* our "you" in our every consideration. If that does not take place, we will find ourselves persecuting God in one form or the other. We will find ourselves opposing God even while we purport to be serving His interests. Saul is not some deliberate atheist, indifferent to God, but a man *zealous* for God. The error that led to the persecution of God's own people, and God Himself *in* His people, was committed by a *religious* man in error, whose "you" was yet *before* God's "Me."

If that basic and fatal error is possible for a man of religious zeal and intention who thought to serve God by seeking opportunity to round up "heretics" in order to bring them back to Jerusalem, how much more, then, are we capable of committing exactly the same error? There is a stubborn, egocentric attitude in us, in whatever form it is expressed, which can only be dislodged by a true conversion.

There is a way in which we filter the word of God through the prism of our own subjectivity, and fit it into the existing framework of our life and categories. We find a way to make the word agreeable to our view of *ourselves* and *our* spirituality. We consciously or unconsciously are habituated to pick and choose what we will hear and apply; what we like or dislike. By so doing, we unknowingly elevate ourselves *above* the word, determining how it is to be fitted comfortably into the categories that we approve. Instead of allowing the word to devastate and demolish our categories, we stand or sit above it as judges, acknowledging and celebrating it *as* the word of God, applauding the speaker for having brought it, and think that by doing so we have done God a service!

This egocentrism is unspeakably deep, especially in the religious realm. What greater disrespect to God, what greater expression of putting our "you" before His "Me," than the way in which we hear and receive the word? He will not share the holy realities of the apostolic faith with those who try to fit them into their existing mindsets. By so doing, we somehow find a way to exalt what the word intends to *devastate*. We set ourselves *above* His word, determining to what degree *we* allow it credence and acceptance.

This may well be the essential malaise of the church and the reason why it is not going from faith to faith and from glory to glory. Our services are abounding with "sermons" rather than the *sent* word of God, which, by its very nature, demands response and change in those who hear it. We should be receiving the word in an open and naked way, letting it have its full work. Are we willing to say with Mary: "May it be done to me according to your word"[3]? Until we come to this place, the word of God can no longer perform the work of God. Mary's posture before the word of God was consequential for her future. For her, it meant nothing less than receiving a pregnancy that could not be explained. On top of that, she was living at a time when unexplained pregnancies received the punishment of death by stoning on the doorstep of the

---

[3] Luke 1:38b

father's house. When Mary said, "May it be done to me according to your word," she meant, "I am willing to bear the full consequence of receiving this word, even if it shall mean my death in disgrace, although I am a virgin in Israel." When God finds a heart like *that*, there is no limit to the extent of the divine work that can be accomplished.

The consequences of receiving the word of God will inevitably lead you to the place of true "death to self." That is how you know that you have received the word. And once you have made *that* reckoning, it will make no difference in what form that death comes. It might be stoning at the doorstep of your father's house, it might be suffering the misunderstanding, the rejection and the reproach of men toward yourself; it might mean physical hazards of all kinds.

> And he said, "Who are you, Lord?" And He said, "I am Jesus whom you are persecuting. [It is hard for you to kick against the goads." So he, trembling and astonished, said, "Lord, what do you want me to do?" Then the Lord said to him, "Arise and go into the city, and you will be told what you must do."][4]
>
> The men who traveled with him stood speechless, hearing the voice but seeing no one. Saul got up from the ground, and though his eyes were open, he could see nothing; and leading him by the hand, they brought him into Damascus. And he was

---

[4] Insert taken from the New King James Version of the Bible, Thomas Nelson Publishers. 1997.

three days without sight, and neither ate nor drank.

Now there was a disciple at Damascus named Ananias; and the Lord said to him in a vision, "Ananias." And he said, "Here I am, Lord." And the Lord said to him, "Get up and go to the street called Straight, and inquire at the house of Judas for a man from Tarsus named Saul, for, he is praying, and he has seen in a vision a man named Ananias come in and lay his hands on him, so that he might regain his sight." But Ananias answered, "Lord, I have heard from many about this man, how much harm he did to Your saints at Jerusalem; and here he has authority from the chief priests to bind all who call on Your name." But the Lord said to him, "Go, for he is a chosen instrument of Mine, to bear My name before the Gentiles and kings and the sons of Israel; for I will show him how much he must suffer for My name's sake."[5]

Saul's answer laid the foundation for his whole apostolic career: "*Lord*, what do *You* want me to do?" Every time we invoke the word "Lord" but do not intend the *remainder* of Saul's statement, we play with a holy thing; we take the Lord's name in vain. Saul's question subsumes and includes every other question. He had no stipulations, no conditions, no reservations, and no requests for illumination, understanding or explanation. If the Lord is Lord, we have but one posture only, to be down on the earth before Him with

---

[5] Acts 9:5-16

this one cry resonating throughout the balance of our natural lives: "*Lord*, what do *You* want me to do?" We need only ask it once, but we live forever in the resonance of that question. And until the Lord hears it, He is not going to tell *you* what to do.

That there are things to do is beyond question; but they can only be performed by those who can be entrusted with His power. The Spirit is given without measure to those who have no purposes in themselves or *for* themselves. They live by one question only: "*Lord*, what do *You* want me to do?" Anything less than this absoluteness is conditional and inadequate. We are released for the works of God when we put before God that thing for which He waits, that thing which He cannot command or compel, but must be utterly and freely and totally given. And no matter what we intone, He is not Lord until it *has* been given.

"*Lord*, what do *You* want me to do?" The answer is eternally the same, though the form of its fulfillment may vary: "I will show him how much he must suffer for My name's sake." No wonder we do not ask the question! How wisely we intuit what the necessary answer must be. But for every suffering that comes as the consequence of obedience to the Lord, there is a glory unspeakable, an eternal reward and a joy even in the midst of distress and trials.

"Who are You, Lord?" God is not going to give the revelation of Himself in truth until He sees a people willing to serve Him in truth. And unless *that* revelation comes, and comes when our faces are upon the ground, what kind of service can we perform? Our service must necessarily reflect whatever our knowledge of God is in truth.

The one who has gone down on his face, who is raised up from it as blind, who can see no man, and must be led away as a child, is the one who is converted. And how many of us want to be *so* led away by the hand? Or do we still have a concern to be understood and perceived in the way we would like men to acknowledge us? Until we are blind to men, even to the spiritual man we think ourselves to be, or who we desire to be known as, we cannot serve God apostolically. We need to come to a place where we see *no* man, even our own man, even our own seeing.

That is why Paul could later say without an iota of presumption: "Follow me as I follow Christ." If we think that Paul's statement is arrogant, it is because we project upon him the ego in which *we* still live, not having fallen on our faces and been blinded by the light of God. We project on Paul our own idea of man, and assume that he must mean by that some kind of egotistic statement. We cannot understand a man who sees no man, and in which the element of self is therefore not a factor. Paul did not need to be recognized. He could be despised, cast out, and become the off-scouring of the world without so much as blinking an eyelid at it; *for he saw no man*. The light that came down, brighter than the noonday sun, blinded him once and for all to that last crippling seeing, even the seeing of ourselves that makes us spiritually self-conscious, and therefore compromised.

"So he, trembling and astonished, said, "Lord, what do You want me to do?" Unless there is trembling and astonishment, we cannot ask that question in truth. You will know your question is authentic when you die a thousand deaths in making it.

Beware of any ultimate surrender that is easy to make, however correct it may be. God waits on that question from us, but it needs to be made from that place of trembling and astonishment because the light of God, the image of God, has brought us down upon our faces. *This* is the point of crossing the Jordan.

In a particular moment of distress or need, many of us have said: "Lord, what do You want me to do?" But who of us has asked it *foundationally* in a once-and-for-all occasion, in utter abandonment of something, never again to be taken back? Once made, those words are irretrievable. Something has been registered and recorded in the annals of heaven. It means you are brought out of that relativistic world of compromise into the "absoluteness" of the kingdom of heaven! Be assured, you will never come up again in the same way. To live a whole life continually reiterating that question *is* true conversion.

What is your condition? What is your status? Are you merely saved, or are you truly *converted?*

The moment God hears your response, He will answer: "Arise and go into the city, and you will be told what you must do." But *before* it is told you, before there is an explanation, before there is any assurance—arise and go. *That* rising is in the strength and power of the resurrection life itself! The rising and the going are a call to things beyond any capacity in ourselves to perform and to do. It is entirely a resurrection requirement! That is what makes apostolic doing a glory, and that is why Paul himself, the chief of the apostles, was the one who most frequently punctuated his prayers with the cry, "Lord, who is sufficient for these things?" God calls us to a dimension of service *beyond* any capacity in ourselves to perform, and says: "Arise and go." And when He says: "Arise," it is not just *an* invitation, but an *impartation of life*. But He waits for the one who has forfeited any hope in himself of serving God on the basis of *his* own ability.

There is no rising, no walking away except in the power of the indestructible life that raised Jesus from the dead, and will raise us also, if we are willing to be struck dead, brought down into that earth and entirely blinded to what we had perceived and celebrated as being correct.

Blind for three days and nights, neither eating nor drinking, Saul reviewed his entire "charismatic" and "evangelical" understanding of the faith. The Lord totally put to death all his biblical understanding; for if he were to be God's gift to the church, he would have to receive an understanding conferred by God.

In keeping with the total dependency to which God had brought Saul, He prepared a simple believer to lay hands on him that he *might* see. From the very inception of his whole apostolic walk, God had to teach the chief apostle the genius and mystery of the Body of Christ, a lesson that many of us have never yet understood, and have not yet seen. It must be conferred by revelation to those who would otherwise be blind to it.

Once you have made this response, it is not for you to deliberate over what your call is, or what you need to do for God. The "arising and going" has its own logic, its own unfolding: "you will be told what you must do." God *will* show us what is required the next day, even the next moment. That is not the way we have been groomed by our society to live. We want to know in advance; we want to have assurance; we want to have a firm grasp on what we are doing, why we are doing it, and what the consequences of our doing will be. But God says: "You will be told what you must do."

There is a necessary cleaving to the God who calls us into an utterness of dependency upon Him. It is a pilgrim way, and you will *never* get used to it. Once you arise and go, you will need to live with the tension of it, just as Abraham did, as every true saint who has ever responded to such a call, because there are things *you* must do. There are things for the kingdom that no one else can do, or is intended to do. And God is bound up for the releasing of it until He has heard your, "Lord, what do You want me to do?" Only then can your purpose and calling be revealed; only then can it be released.

"Saul got up from the ground, and though his eyes were open, he could see nothing." From that moment onwards, he only had regard for God. Everything was for the Lord's sake rather than his own. What kind of church would we have today if people of *this* kind were in its fellowships? They would be those who labor selflessly day and night, bringing the whole counsel of God, living continually in the resonance of that one great statement: "Lord, what do You want me to do?"

Many are called, but few are chosen. Many saved, but few are converted. Conversion is to the uttermost, *or it is not conversion*. It is an utterness of spirit toward God. The world cannot abide the truly converted, and will forever oppose them. But the works that the converted will do are eternal in their consequences.

So, in the name of Jesus, and as the minister of this word, I call upon you to respond. Bring down to earth every lesser thing, however correct, however applauded by men, however much it delights your own soul, that *He* might raise you up for the works that *you* must do, when you arise and go in the power of His resurrection life. Let God hear you utter that one statement in truth: "Lord, what do You want me to do?"

OTHER BOOKS by Art Katz

REALITY: THE HOPE OF GLORY
The four messages in this book are a powerful inspiration to those who will not settle for less than the true meaning of life as a disciple of Christ. Paperback, 156 pages.

THE SPIRIT OF TRUTH
Into this age of religious pretension, exaggeration and deception, Art brings a deep, incisive probing into the nature of truth. Every lover and guardian of truth will find this an insightful and demanding book. Paperback, 101 pages.

BEN ISRAEL – ODYSSEY OF A MODERN JEW
Written as a literal journal, Art recounts his experience as an atheist and former Marxist being apprehended by a God whom he was not seeking. The message of this book has been powerfully used to bring other of Art's Jewish kinsmen to the faith of their fathers. Paperback, 149 pages.

THE ANATOMY OF DECEPTION
In a dark and seductive age, and one that is increasingly abounding in deception and lying signs, the ability to discern between the false and the true is of paramount importance. Paperback, 60 pages.

THE TEMPTATIONS OF CHRIST – *A Call to Sonship and Maturity*

The scriptures indicate that Jesus was led into the wilderness in the *fullness* of the Spirit, but came out of that testing place in the *power* of the Spirit. The author examines the necessary progression in our Christian lives without which we will never be able to convey the knowledge of the risen Christ. Paperback, 56 pages.

WHAT A JEW DOES WITH JESUS

Despite the apparent contradiction, the author pleads with his Jewish kinsmen to take into their deepest consideration the truth that biblical Judaism is determined solely by what we do with Jesus of Nazareth. Paperback, 128 pages.

TRUE FELLOWSHIP – *Church as Community*

When God called us to establish a Christian community, I knew that it was a call to the cross, to humiliation and suffering. We were going to be living closely and intensively with other believers on a daily basis in which our defects, our shortcomings and our failures would be revealed. Out of the agonies and the joys, we gave opportunity for a reality to come forth that can best be described as "true fellowship." Paperback, 146 pages.

THE PROPHETIC CALL – *True and False Prophets*

If we cannot distinguish between the prophets that are true and those that are false, it is a statement that we are unable to distinguish between the God who is true and the god who is false. Art seeks to identify the essential elements of what makes a prophet true, and by that, he gives a corresponding glimpse into the truth of God as He in fact is. Paperback, 110 pages.

THE HOLOCAUST: WHERE WAS GOD? – *An inquiry into the biblical roots of tragedy.*

In a daring hypothesis, the author turns to the ancient Hebrew scriptures as the key of interpretation to one of the most catastrophic events of modern times: the Jewish Holocaust of World War II. In this examination of that ultimate tragedy, the issue of God *as God* is brought courageously to the forefront of our modern consideration as few books have attempted to do. Paperback, 91 pages.